# DOUBLE EXPOSURE

## Take Four

Compiled and Photographed
by
Roddy McDowall

WILLIAM MORROW AND COMPANY, INC.
New York

**Library of Congress Cataloging-in-Publication Data**

McDowall, Roddy.
    Double exposure, take four / compiled and photographed by Roddy McDowall.
        p.    cm.
        Includes index.
        ISBN 0-888-11309-5
        1. Entertainers—Portraits.    2. Entertainers—Biography.
    3. Celebrities—Portraits.    4. Celebrities—Biography.    I. Title.
    PN1583.M365    1993
    791'.092'2—dc20
        [B]                                                     92-43984
                                                                  CIP

Printed in Japan

First Edition

1   2   3   4   5   6   7   8   9   10

BOOK DESIGN BY DAVID CHARLSEN

# Contents

*for my sister, Virginia*

A Gallery of the Celebrated
with commentary by
the Equally Celebrated

# Annie Potts
## BY
# Tim Curry

This is a woman with the courage of her convictions and of her contradictions. Beautiful, generous, loyal, and funny. She is possessed of extraordinary compassion—a compassion she extends to the characters she plays and which lends them their vigorous, rigorous interior light.

As an actress, she breaks my heart; as a friend, she nourishes it.

# Tom Courtenay
## BY
# Peter Medak

Tom Courtenay is the most sensitive, wondrous acting talent I have ever had the good fortune to direct. It's like driving a Rolls-Royce.

His soul, or rather the soul of his characters, just reaches out through those wonderful eyes. Soft, funny, touching and sad. He is pure cinema magic.

*Brentwood, California    1964*

# Jessie Matthews

## BY

# Anna Lee

Enchanting little Jessie! Floating across the stage . . . light as thistle-down . . . the wonderful legs soaring as high as those of a ballerina . . . no wonder she was known as the "Dancing Divinity"! I was fifteen or sixteen years old when I first saw her in London in a Charlot Revue, and I adored her from that moment on.

It was not until 1935 that I worked with her in *First a Girl* (re-made in Hollywood some fifty years later, under the title of *Victor/Victoria* with Julie Andrews in Jessie's part.) We made *First a Girl* partly on location in the South of France, and during those halcyon days I came to know Jessie quite well. At that time she was married to Sonnie Hale, and even then I sensed her insecurity, resulting from the misery and guilt she had suffered in 1930 when she had fallen in love with Sonnie and he had divorced his wife, Evelyn Laye, in order to marry her. Jessie was named co-respondent and during the court proceedings, which must have been an agony for her, she was called an "adulteress" and a "husband-stealer." The fact that Evelyn Laye was a very popular and well-loved actress made Jessie's position all the worse in the eyes of the public, resulting in a temporary halt to her career and causing psychological scars which remained with her for the rest of her life.

After I left England in 1939, I lost touch with Jessie but continued to follow reports of her career. At one time she was supposed to come to America to make a film with Fred Astaire, which had always been her dream. Evidently Sonnie Hale decided against it, which caused her great unhappiness. The marriage was already in trouble, and finally ended in divorce. In the early forties she came to New York to do a Broadway show, but before it opened she had a nervous breakdown, the first of many. During the years that followed, she gallantly continued to work, in spite of ill-health and a slumping career.

I did not see her again until 1979, when she came to Hollywood and appeared in concert at the Mayfair Music Hall in Santa Monica. By this time she was in her seventies . . . plump and white-haired but with the piquant elfin personality and those huge magical eyes that I remembered so well. She no longer danced, but the voice, though husky at times, was still sweet and harmonious. Accompanied by the incomparable Michael Feinstein, she sang many of her old hit songs, including *Dancing on the Ceiling, Over My Shoulder* and her own brave version of *My Way.*

*Studio City, California*      1979

I loved and admired her, not only for her talent as a performer but for her indomitable courage . . . her refusal to accept defeat in the face of overwhelming misfortune . . . disastrous marriages . . . a constant struggle with ill-health, and the tragic but inevitable decline of a career that had started so brilliantly. She never gave up, and continued to work until the end of her life. Throughout all the hardships, she never lost her sense of humour, nor her fierce loyalty to those friends who stayed by her side.

Shortly after her appearance at the Mayfair Music Hall, she returned to England. When we said good-bye, she confided to me that she would soon be coming back to Hollywood to make a picture with her idol, Fred Astaire, with whom she had always longed to work. "Of course," she said, "we are both older now . . . but we could still play two elderly dancers, re-living their former successes . . . " I rather think this was wishful thinking on her part, for I believe she knew even then that she was suffering from the cancer that took her life some two years later.

Dear Jessie! I like to think that now, at last, her dream has come true and that, with Fred Astaire, she is "dancing on the ceiling" of some celestial sphere.

❏

# Jules Feiffer
## BY
# Nora Ephron

He looks very benign, doesn't he? The cigar is an attempt in the other direction, but it fools no one; the overall effect is utterly benign. And this is what he is like: he is kind, sweet, dear, darling Jules. It seems to me that of all the writers I know, he is the only one whose disposition and personality are almost completely different from his work. You go to his plays—brilliant, angry, savagely funny—and it's virtually impossible to imagine that your friend Jules has written them. His weekly cartoon strip is as full of wit and rage at the people running this country as it was back in the Fifties, when we all became Feiffer fans for life. He hangs in, and nothing gets past him, nothing—no President, no movement, no young woman in black tights. Jules once wrote that he always wanted to be Fred Astaire, but I prefer to think of him as Phil Rizzuto: he is the shortstop of life.

*New York City*     *1990*

# Moss Hart
## BY
# Kitty Carlisle

I was once asked during a television interview what I like most about Moss and I said— *everything*.

I found him endlessly diverting and stimulating. He made me laugh, which was irresistible. He found me funny, which was even more irresistible. His wit was gentle, never hurtful, and he was a wonderful listener.

Moss was a writer and he loved to give me presents he could write on. One Valentine's Day he gave me a gold heart inscribed: "I love little Kitty/her coat is so warm/and if you don't kick her/she'll do you no harm."

For our sixth wedding anniversary a gold disk for my bracelet: "What larks, my darling, what larks!"

*New York City*     *1956*

# Libby Holman
## BY
# Robert Lewis

Remembrances of Libby . . .

My first meeting with her was when Ralph Holmes, a young actor in my Theatre Workshop, asked if his wife could take class, too.

"Who is she?" I asked.

"Libby Holman."

Like everyone else I had read the many newspaper accounts of the death of her first husband, Smith Reynolds, the twenty-one-year-old heir to the Reynolds tobacco fortune, by a shot fired into his head in the early morning of July 6, 1932 at Reynolda, the family's estate in Winston-Salem, North Carolina. Opinions differed as to whether Smith committed suicide or if Libby was culpable.

I also remembered well her smokey voice in such musical revues as *The Little Show* and *Three's a Crowd*, torching numbers like "Moanin' Low," "Body and Soul" and "Can't We Be Friends?" Critic Mason Brown called her "The Flagstad of the Blues."

I said, "Sure. Bring her along."

Ralph and Libby prepared a scene from some drawing room comedy and presented it in class. When it was over, I remarked that they did well but the material was not very challenging for them. I suggested that class was a place where an actor should take chances and stretch himself. Turning to Libby I said, "Why not try something with some real drama in it, maybe a scene from a play about a woman killing her husband?"

Before the words were out of my mouth, and with my heart pounding, I said to myself, "Don't panic, Bobby. Don't apologize. Keep talking."

I went on. "Why not try the Jeanne Eagels part in *The Letter* where the woman kills the lover, insisting he was trying to rape her, when actually it was because he had a Chinese mistress and . . . "

"All right. All right," interrupted Libby, "I'll do it."

*Ogunquit, Maine     1954*

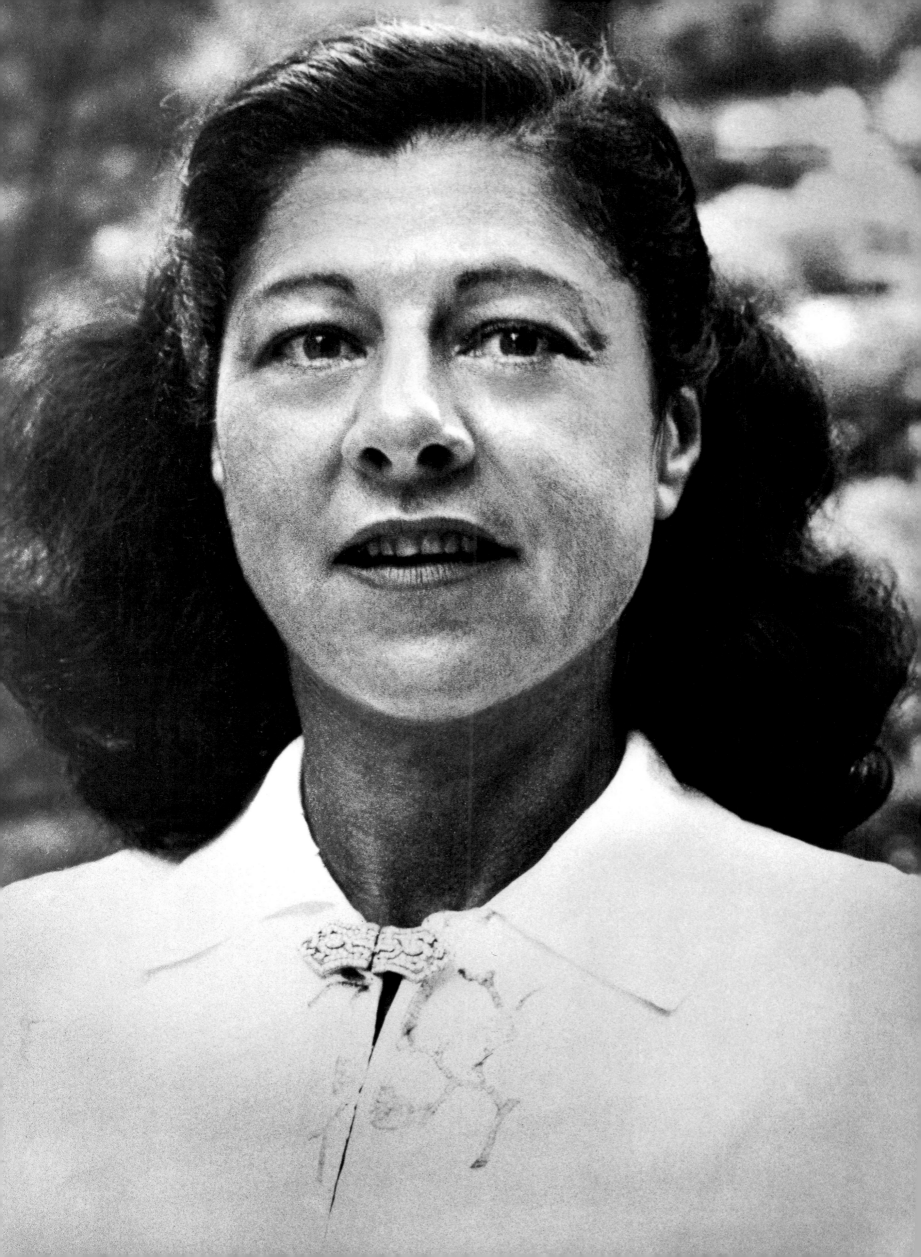

The day Libby was to present the scene in class, I prepared myself carefully so as not to make another gaffe when I had to give my criticism.

I must have been over-rehearsed, because I heard myself saying that the shooting of the lover wasn't quite believable. I even got up to show her how to handle the gun more convincingly.

I was sure I'd never see her in class again. Wrong. She couldn't have been more understanding and invited me up for a week-end at Treetops, her estate in Stamford, Connecticut. We became fast friends and I occupied my room with the light green wallpaper in her house for many weekends to come.

In 1942 I directed *Mexican Mural* in which Libby played a leading role and sang a couple of Mexican songs beautifully. The male lead was Montgomery Clift, and in this production they met and solidified what was to become an enduring friendship.

Never was there a woman of such contrasts as Libby. She had no single perfect feature, yet all added up to a creature of sensuality and, yes, glamour. Although she was stalked by a series of unnatural deaths throughout her life, she remained a generous, bright, witty, often downright funny friend. Among my favorites around her pool on weekends were Jane and Paul Bowles, Oliver Smith, Dawn Powell, Constance Collier, Tennessee Williams and Gore Vidal (she called him Gorvy, as in Gorvy Doll).

Heavy drinking parties were contrasted with lovely evenings when Libby would turn on Flagstad recordings and read aloud the short stories of Katherine Anne Porter. Quite political, Libby was on a committee with Katherine Anne and Dorothy Parker to re-elect Roosevelt for President. Libby said Mrs. Parker turned to her once and said of the very handsome Katherine Anne, "Look at her. She looks just like Mrs. Harrison Williams, if Mrs. Harrison Williams could read and write."

Among the strange deaths Libby survived were those of Phillips Holmes, her boyfriend, in an airplane disaster; his brother Ralph, whom she married—from an overdose of sleeping pills; her dear friend, Jeanne Eagels, of heroin; Monty Clift—it was called a heart attack; her teenage son by Smith Reynolds, Topper, who fell in an amateur attempt to climb Mt. Whitney; and, of course, Smith, of a gun wound to his temple.

The tragic story ended when Libby was found, clad in a bikini, slumped over the front seat of her Rolls-Royce in the garage at Treetops. She was cremated and her ashes strewn over her glorious daffodil beds.

❏

# The ABC's of John Ritter
## BY
# Blake Edwards

**A**ctor

**B**edeviled

**C**lown

**D**elinquent

**E**rogenous

**F**ickle

**G**entle

**H**edonist

**I**nsatiable

**J**ester

**K**issable

**L**ovable

**M**ischievous

**N**udist

**O**ptimist

**P**essimist

**Q**uixotic

**R**omantic

**S**atyr

**T**ruant

**U**nique

**V**exatious

**W**icked

**X**-rated

**Y**enta

**Z**orro (with his fly unbuttoned)

*Los Angeles*          *1988*

# Lou Gossett, Jr.
## BY
# Sidney Poitier

For standing at the gate when enemies were close at hand. For speaking words of comfort in places where hope has lost its meaning. For lending your strength to whoever is willing to try just one more time. And, for always remembering Africa.

Thank you.

*Studio City, California*      *1992*

# Ann Miller
## BY
# Van Johnson

I first met Ann Miller at RKO Studios when we were making *Too Many Girls*. She introduced me to many stars who were working on the lot—Carole Lombard, Orson Welles, Charles Laughton, Kay Francis, etc. She was a big booster of mine. We didn't meet again till we did a *Love Boat* special with Ethel Merman, Carol Channing, Della Reese, and Cab Calloway. Then we were both fortunate in appearing in the last of the great industrial shows staged by the Miliken Family—Alexis Smith, Gloria Swanson, Ann, and myself at the Waldorf Astoria. Little did she know that a producer named Harry Rigby was watching one day and proceeded to change her life. He saw that she stopped the show twice daily and decided to put her and Mickey Rooney together in *Sugar Babies* which they played for years here and in London. It made her rich. I hear she just bought Arizona. It couldn't happen to a nicer lady! They don't make 'em like that *anymore*!

*Los Angeles*        *1991*

# Thornton Wilder
## BY
# Elia Kazan

Dear Roddy:

At the time I was directing *The Skin of Our Teeth*, its author was in the U.S. Army. As I recall, he appeared at rehearsals twice. The first time for the usual palaver of good wishes which launch a production. The second was on a more serious mission. I was having a discipline problem with Tallulah Bankhead and had lost sympathy (and touch) with her. Thornton happened to be in New York and I thought he might help me. He came to the theatre, saw the show, then went into her dressing room and apparently had a jolly visit with the old girl, for, sitting at the back of the "house," where I was waiting for Thornton, I heard laughter and purple language. He came out after an hour and a half and left the theatre through the stage door without a word to me. Needless to say the lady's behavior was even worse in the days that followed. I saw that I had to solve the problem in my own way. How I did is told in my book, *A Life* (Knopf), along with other incidents relating to Miss Bankhead.

I admired *Skin of Our Teeth* as well as *Our Town*. But to tell the unvarnished truth, the fondest memories I have of Thornton are as a master of the intellectual bull session. He'd invite a group of students (among them myself at one time) to sit with him and talk about the great figures of literature with whom he had an intimate acquaintance. He didn't reduce them to common humanity, he raised them to common humanity. The men and women he talked about were like us, passionately struggling to express what was most intimate in their selves, sometimes succeeding, sometimes failing. Thornton brought them close. He was the greatest conversationalist on the theme of the artist and his work that I have ever heard, with the possible exception of Harold Clurman. The charming thing about Thornton's talks was the understanding he expressed for each of his subjects as human beings. By an excursion into hero-worship, he fired us all to exceed ourselves. We left those sessions full of hope and desire and possibly better artists.

Roddy, no cuts are to be made in the preceding; all or nothing.

With my best regards,

*Elia*

*New York City        1953*

# Mel Gibson
## BY
# Richard Donner

Mel Gibson? One word: *Melisms*—or at least that's what we called them on the set. Never have I met anyone with such a cleverly twisted take on the English language—and *funny*. The guy's truly a delight to be around.

I don't want to compare him to Cary Grant, Jimmy Stewart, Gary Cooper, John Wayne, Spencer Tracy, or Humphrey Bogart . . . but these are just a few I could if I would, but I won't.

I treasure his friendship.

*Studio City, California*        *1991*

# Annabella
## BY
# Cesar Romero

Annabella was France's gift to Hollywood. I met this divine lady when she was married to my dear friend Tyrone Power. As an actress, she brought beauty and a vibrant, sparkling personality to the screen. She cut her career short to devote herself to being a full-time wife. Their beautiful home was the gathering place of the rich and famous, as well as the *not* so rich and famous. Always a gracious hostess, she had the affection and admiration of all who knew her. She eventually returned to France where she now lives. She makes occasional visits here, but not nearly enough to satisfy her many friends who miss her.

*Beverly Hills*     *1990*

# Shelley Duvall
## BY
# Robert Altman

When I first saw her, she had painted long eyelashes on her face, and I thought, "Here is a girl who is trying to make me think she is a Raggedy Ann doll." It was only years later that I realized that she WAS a Raggedy Ann doll.

*Los Angeles     1979*

# Luciano Pavarotti
## BY
# Beverly Sills

Smiling face, sad eyes, white handkerchief, scarf, warm, funny, venerable, vulnerable, unique, *simpatico*, colleague, friend, hugger, kisser, voice, voice, voice heart-grabbing. Pavarotti.

# Robert Wise
## BY
# Nina Foch

For so many of the last thirty-seven years, a particular bunch of pals would gather at Bob Wise's house, for Christmas, New Year, Easter, the Fourth of July, and countless other times. Warm, happy times. And wonderful food! (I dream of it still!)

Bob is the best pal of all.

With our respective mates, he and I have done so many interesting things. We've been to master classes together. He even took me to the gas chamber at San Quentin to research *I Want to Live*. He has put up with me through boyfriends, husbands, the birth of my son, divorces, illnesses—never critical, always supportive. You couldn't have a better friend.

Nor one of whom you could be more proud. I mean, he edited *Citizen Kane.* He has directed so many films. Among them: *The Set-up, Executive Suite, West Side Story*, and *Sound of Music*. He is shy. He is sensitive. He has marvelous insight. I adored working with him.

All things considered, Bob Wise is an excellent man.

*Beverly Hills      1960*

# Natalie Wood
## BY
# Maureen Stapleton

Natalie is every great song
in the world, starting with
"The Most Beautiful Girl."

# Karl Malden
## BY
# Hume Cronyn

From *The Streets of San Francisco* to the shores of Tripoli you can't find a better actor, a nicer man, a more generous spirit. I'm talking about our President . . . the President of the Academy of Motion Picture Arts and Sciences that is, Mr. Karl Malden. (Wild applause here punctuated by a roll of drums.)

I refuse to dwell on his professional credits except for one: He was the best damn Ephraim Cabot in O'Neill's *Desire Under the Elms* that I ever hope to see—and most of you missed that one and are poorer for it.

Born March 14, 1914, in Gary, Indiana, Mladen Sukilovich was of Yugoslav parentage and worked for a time in one of Gary's "satanic" steel mills. He married Mona about 52 years ago, and neither of them could have been more fortunate.

Karl and Mona, Jessica and I met in 1947 when, with Marlon B. and Kim Hunter, Karl and Jess were appearing together in that play about a streetcar. "The kindness of strangers" (Karl and Mona) was never more apparent. We have been close friends ever since.

Ladies and gentlemen, I have no cute little anecdotes to offer, but I give you Karl Malden: dedicated, loyal, warm hearted (his bark being worse than his bite), kind and, oh yes, a pretty fair actor, director, teacher and Executive—or do I repeat myself? I'm proud to be an intimate friend.

# Leslie Caron
## BY
# Jack Larson

Leslie Caron didn't want to become a movie star. Her training and ambitions were in ballet. Early on she had a success in Paris for Roland Petit in a ballet he created for her and Jean Babilee called *The Sphinx*. Then came the offer from Gene Kelly and M.G.M. to co-star in *An American in Paris*, and she didn't want to do it. Her American mother insisted that Leslie should go to Hollywood and be in the movie, and Leslie, being a very well brought up and disciplined daughter, did as her mother wished. She wasn't happy about it.

When we first met in 1951 at Debbie Reynolds' swimming pool, I was even unhappier than Leslie, feeling trapped playing Jimmy Olsen in the *Superman* television series. Our unhappiness brought us together. We went everywhere in drab clothes, Leslie usually dressed in black and I mainly in shades of Brooks Brothers' gray. Many years later, when we were both older and happy and dressed colorfully in Jamaica, I looked at Leslie, recalled our drab youthful look and said, "What were we doing then?" Leslie replied, "Like the characters in Chekhov, my dear, we were in mourning for our lives."

Leslie needn't have mourned. She's had and has a marvelous life. The key word I'd choose to describe her is resilient (beside glamorous, loving, gifted, tasteful, homemaker [her children Christopher and Jennifer always said their mother "had a way with chocolate"], adventurous). To remain a star and become increasingly beautiful over four decades in an entertainment world certain to be full of ups and downs takes great resiliency. Leslie worked to become a brilliant film actress, returned twice to the world of ballet, became a triumphant stage actress, became a writer of short stories *(Revenge)* and screen-plays, one of which she's poised to direct in France.

Throughout the years, she's been self-critical, direct, and honest to others. On a disastrous opening night of a ballet she was in in New York City, caused by a lack of time for scenery rehearsals and a refusal by the management to postpone because a glamorous opening night party couldn't be rescheduled, when others involved were agreeing with their impresario, Sol

*Culver City, California*     *1959*

Hurok, who said "it couldn't have been helped, it was no one's fault," Leslie told him, "It was your fault, Mr. Hurok. We had this unfortunate premiere because you wouldn't postpone this party."

Her friend Jean Renoir, for whom she performed two of his plays, said of her, "If my father had known Leslie, he would have painted her all his days."

As for her film career that she began so unwillingly: once, some years ago, she and I were in a restaurant that employed a violin ensemble. When the musicians recognized her, they began to play themes from her famous films. The music went on and on from *American in Paris, Lili, Gigi, Daddy Longlegs, Fanny.*

The beautiful music goes on, and so does Leslie Caron.

❏

# Brad Pitt
## BY
# Roy London

The actor's challenge:
to struggle and break through, only to struggle again;
to struggle to find his gifts,
to struggle to embody his gifts,
to struggle to remain true to his gifts and not squander them,
to play with the possibilities,
to go beyond the formed and proven,
to rattle the status quo, propelling himself and us,
crying and laughing, into the future.

Some are born to surrender to this struggle,
this divine, rough journey.
They are blessed.
Their restlessness makes anything possible.

I saw this in Brad the moment he stood up to work in my studio.

*Norwalk, California*    *1988* (page 55)
*Studio City, California*    *1992*

# Ann Blyth
## BY
# Jane Withers

Ann Blyth and I have been friends for over forty years. She radiates beauty from within in everything she ever does. She is truly one of God's dearest blessings.

*Burbank, California*     *1990*

# Tim Burton
## BY
# Vincent Price

There's got to be a name to go with this face . . . what a face! . . . something sad, serious, but about to laugh at himself . . . comic with a kind of sublimated astonishment at being photographed for a book of celebrities. When you get to know the person behind this enchanted face, you know it's just what Tim Burton should look like. He not only looks like this but also speaks like he looks, thinks that way, and, in every way, is a completely enchanting person of great talent and humanity. I've known him since his beginnings in a business that took a properly short time to recognize his genius, and we all have a long way to go with Tim, thank God.

# Alfred de Liagre, Jr.
## BY
# Robert Whitehead

My first connection with Delly was many years ago, one in which I felt a distinct hostility. I was on the point of signing a contract to produce Giraudoux's *The Madwoman of Chaillot*. The proceedings were delayed for a day or two in which time, with some agency manipulating, the script wound up in the hands of Delly. That he was competing was perfectly reasonable—that he won seemed to me perfectly unreasonable, so it took a year or two for me to view Delly as a talented, companionable colleague and, eventually, as the years went by, as a friend who was a warm, lively raconteur and an extremely witty fellow.

The last time I saw Delly was very shortly before his death in the spring of 1987. He was walking slowly west on 44th Street, carrying a file under his arm. He was very bent over; he looked ill, old and ravaged. He was completely disinterested in discussing his condition, but observed that working in the Broadway theatre at this moment in history was an insanity. He burst out laughing, rather hopelessly, and went on his way shaking his head and still laughing.

We all know that Delly could be fun and was certainly socially acceptable. But what I think he would like to hear, and what happens to be the truth, is that he was a tasteful, tough-minded, top-flight producer and he is badly needed in the Broadway scene today.

*New York City        1953*

ALFRED de LIAGRE JR and ROGER L. STEVENS
with RODNEY ACKLAND present

BRIAN          URSULA
AHERNE         JEANS
in
Escapade
A Comedy by ROGER MacDOUGALL

MELVILLE COOPER
MARJORY MALLIE          MURRAY MATHESON
FELIX DEEBANK           REX THOMPSON
RODDY McDOWALL
Direction by MR de LIAGRE
Production Designed by DONALD ŒNSLAGER

atinee To a

# Rachel Roberts
## BY
# Lindsay Anderson

I first met Rachel when her then husband, Alan Dobie, was acting in my production of *Serjeant Musgrave's Dance* at the Royal Court. In the programme notes about the cast, I had written that Alan was married to "the actress, Rachel Roberts." Rachel was outside the theatre before the first preview, leafing through the programme. She shrieked delightedly when she saw her name. "The actress, Rachel Roberts! . . . *the* actress! . . ." I recognized and immediately warmed to her joyous mixture of send-up, self send-up and huge, astonished pleasure. That was Rachel, ardent and outrageous, in the days before awards and fame and recognition by taxi-drivers. She was simpler then, and happier.

That was also before my friend Karel Reisz, with such brilliant perception, cast her as the discontented, passionate, thwarted Brenda in *Saturday Night and Sunday Morning*. Rachel showed in that how she could respond when her material and her direction were first-class. She was a terrific actress: she would dare anything. Her emotional power could be frightening, self-lacerating. At first, I admit, I doubted that she was right for the bitter, walled-up Mrs. Hammond in *This Sporting Life*. But it was exactly the pressure of violent temperament under implacable control that created that unforgettable performance.

Rachel of course was not English; she was Celt, totally Welsh. And of all the Celts, it is the Welsh who find it most difficult to deal with the cool of the Anglo-Saxons, their unquestioning assumption of superiority, their distaste for temperament. The English theatre could not accommodate Rachel, nor could the English cinema. She scared them. And then she had to fall for Rex, who brought with him all that establishment charm and class, all that champagne and caviar and shirts from Jermyn Street. Everything that wasn't Rachel, but to which she obstinately insisted on aspiring.

*Crowborough, Sussex*     *1966*

When she was young she wanted to look like Hedy Lamarr. She had such distinction in the little black dress I would try to make her wear, but she never lost her yearning for fish-net tights. She knew her weaknesses and she laughed at them, but she would still surrender to them. Perhaps she never quite believed in her success; or it was not the kind of success she longed for. We tried to stop her. *"Rachel . . . !"* But we couldn't.

She would sometimes say, "I wish you'd known me earlier. I was good fun then. Not all messed up, the way I am now." She was messed up, and none of us, friends and hangers-on and foolish doctors alike, could pull her out of it. And yet—what laughs we had! She was one of life's incandescents. Irreplaceable.

❑

# John Guare
## BY
# Brooke Hayward

John Guare has many legitimate claims to fame, but none of them can hold a candle to his talent as a travel companion. Without Guare's untimely intervention, for example, he, his wife Adele and I would never have had the opportunity to be detained for five hours in a top-security Egyptian Army camp situated somewhere in the desert between the pyramids of Saqqâra and Giza. That the three of us were expected momentarily at a black-tie dinner in honor of Mrs. Sadat, given by the American Ambassador and his wife, was of no concern to our captors, who were quite convinced we were spies.

My husband, Peter Duchin, and myself, and the Guares, traveling together around Egypt for the previous ten days, had avidly accepted an invitation from Farouk Younes, a charming entrepreneur we'd met at a party in Cairo, to accompany him on horseback for an afternoon gallop across the sands. It happened that Farouk, who'd single-handedly revived the sport of polo in Egypt (although played there since the twelfth century, it had fallen out of favor during the Nasser years), owned a string of Arabian polo ponies which he stabled on his farm out by Saqqâra. Learning that the beauteous Adele and I were competent horsewomen, he had proposed that we ride the thirteen miles from one set of pyramids to the other and back again in time for tea. Before we could blink, our husbands jumped on the bandwagon, so to speak, followed quickly by our friend, Frank Wizner, then American Ambassador to the country. Lo and behold we were suddenly an expedition, for Wizner was not allowed to brush his teeth without his trusty team of bodyguards in attendance.

Now, as it happened, there was one amongst us who had never before been on a horse: John Guare. He was so eager, however, that we all saddled up and set off as if we had a budding Eddie Arcaro in our midst. This was a hideous mistake; within ten minutes he began to develop saddle sores and lag behind. In sympathy, first Adele, then I, and finally Major Hilmi, Frank Wizner's bodyguard, dropped back to cheer him up. Needless to say, the Ambassador, Farouk and my husband, Peter, all raced on without glancing back. We never saw them again.

After plodding ahead through the desert for several hours (foolishly expecting the others to return for us at any moment), I pointed at the setting sun and suggested we reverse direction. Major Hilmi had another idea: he knew a less treacherous route home which simply required turning north toward the paved road. Thus we rode straight into the barbed wire of a vast army encampment.

Swarms of young Egyptian soldiers in camouflage fatigues and thonged sandals rushed toward us. I suggested that we make a run for it, but Major Hilmi nervously pointed out that Guare could barely proceed at a walk. Of course, once the soldiers spotted Major Hilmi's gun

and walkie-talkie, they became terribly agitated; words were exchanged, incomprehensible to us Americans, then we were surrounded and—still astride our Arabian steeds—paraded, as it were, down the main road of the barracks, in orderly formation: first a sort of raggle-taggle honor guard, then Adele and I on a pair of matched white ponies, and clip-clopping along right behind us, Guare and Major Hilmi.

John Guare was transformed by the unexpected drama. "Look! Look!" he kept exclaiming. "Isn't this just amazing?" He smiled with pleasure and waved excitedly down at the uniformed youths who were materializing from every direction, running alongside us and calling out to each other in Arabic.

And it was amazing, because it happened to be the exact moment when the sun sank into the desert and the moon arose out of it, the ritual moment of evening prayer. All around us the amplified cries of muezzins filled the air, mingled with horses' hoof beats and the guttural buzzing of soldiers. Adele's long dark hair had come unknotted and was streaming down her back. Overcome with emotion, John triumphantly whipped a camera from his khaki vest pocket and before Major Hilmi could stop him, began recording the scene for posterity. Flash! Flash! went the camera in the fading light. That did it (in conjunction with the gun and walkie-talkie).

Hours later, the Ambassador's armored van roared into the encampment, disgorging Wizner, bodyguards, Peter Duchin and our host (whose main concern was the welfare of his horses, which I found very engaging). It seems that Hilmi's walkie-talkie had finally made contact with those of the other guards back on Farouk's roof where everyone was enjoying a delicious tea and watching the sunset. By the time our release was finally negotiated, Guare was in a state of ecstasy. And for days afterwards every detail was savored, from the confiscated film to our breakneck drive back into Cairo to our bedraggled appearance in riding clothes at the dinner for Mrs. Sadat.

I have no doubt that someday I shall encounter these details again in some form or other, probably surreal, certainly humorous, but unmistakenly drawn by the magic pen of the great traveler himself.

*Beverly Hills*        *1990*

# Luchino Visconti
## BY
# Dirk Bogarde

The cabin-trunk was a splendid affair. Beautifully crafted in olive-green leather. Lined in watered silk of the same colours, embellished with the initials of Gustav von Aschenbach in gothic-gold.

The drawers were fitted with every kind of bottle and pomade-pot, all in heavy crystal, all engraved, all silver stoppered. The mirrors and the hairbrushes were silver backed, coat hangers swung gently in quilted silk to match the lining. The locks and hinges were polished, hand-forged brass. No one would ever see this splendour, in all probability, for it was only to be used once in the gondola or while it was being carried by porters to von Aschenbach's apartment in the Hotel des Bains. That was all.

I remember saying, in amazed bewilderment, "But Luchino!" (I was by this time permitted to use his Christian name.) "So much glory! Who will ever see it?" His eyes, those fine, hooded, black-agate eyes regarded me with a flick of irritation at my crassness.

"You," he said.

And, as usual, he was right. I did see it. I knew it, was very aware of it at all times throughout the work ahead. That cabin-trunk stood for the complete background of the man I was to play. Elegant, expensive, luxurious, spoiled, vain, fastidious, correct, slightly old-maidish too. Everything in its place. It was expected of me, this background, and like so many apparently minute and worthless extravagant details, it embellished the work I offered him.

He was not incorrect in supplying me with such a fund of detail, so much valuable instruction. I learned from the cabin-trunk. It was the only thing I ever received by way of "motivation." We never discussed the part of von Aschenbach again. It was all there before me, as clear as clear.

That was Visconti the Director.

As dead today as the Brontosaurus. Poor actors . . .

*Palermo, Italy      1962*

# Margaret O'Brien
## BY
# Sylvia Fine Kaye

Lionel Barrymore used to say that Metro had an acting factory in the person of five-year-old Margaret O'Brien. He called her Sarah Bernhardt. Actually, little Miss O'Brien was such a formidable actress that, unlike other child stars, she never seemed to be acting at all.

When she was heartbroken, I was heartbroken, when she was happy I was happy. And in addition to all of this, she had a magic of her own that gave everything she did an ineffable glow.

Was I a fan? You bet!

*Studio City, California*      *1990*

# Peter Martins
## BY
# Richard Thomas

Peter Martins—the quintessence of the Bournonville style, whose embodiment of that technique was perhaps most elegantly manifested in his performance of James in the ballet *La Sylphide*. In that characterization his power and personality as a performer were married to the self-effacing virtues of the true *danseur noble*.

From this to the cool abstractions of Balanchine, in whose repertoire he likewise excelled, and under whose guidance grew into an American ballet eminence as dancer, choreographer and, finally, as artistic leader of the New York City Ballet.

*New York City        1965*

# Kitty Carlisle
## BY
# George Axelrod

When Mike Nichols told Groucho Marx he'd seen *A Night at the Opera* seventeen times, Groucho was flattered until Mike explained that what he adored about the picture was the love story. Although Mike may have been speaking, at least partially, in jest, I chose to take him literally. Not only that, but I am in total agreement!

How many times have I myself squirmed through the dreary antics of those three *buffoons* (even the benighted *Zeppo* refused to play in *this* one!), watching, in white-knuckled tension, as the wondrous and beautiful Kitty Carlisle struggles bravely, but in vain, to bring at least a *shred* of dignity, a *glimmer* of seriousness, and (yes!), of *culture* to the whole grotesque proceedings!

"They told me I was to wear beautiful clothes and sing Grand Opera!" Kitty sobs. "I closed my eyes," she continues, reaching daintily for yet another Kleenex, "and *pretended* not to notice what was going on *around* me! *You are slumming*, I told myself again and again! How was one to know the wretched thing would become a classic?"

Kitty Carlisle Hart! Three magical words—nine magical lives! Born, Grand Duchess Anastasia! Believed by some to have been executed by the Bolsheviki, but, in fact, rescued by the Shuberts and smuggled to Broadway where she achieved instant stardom! On to Hollywood (into each life a little rain must fall!) and degradation at the hands of the brothers Marx! Rescued again, this time by Prince Charming himself—disguised (for tax reasons) as a lowly playwright! Truly, a fairy-tale life! One a-bristle (as you can see!) with exclamation points!

Now, in the sixth or seventh (who would be so vulgar as to count?) of her many enchanted lives, she runs, velvet hand concealed within an iron glove, New York State Arts Council, bringing (as it were) culture to Albany in the Nineties! Philistine legislators from Utica and even *Syracuse* are but Silly Putty in her hands, pouring tax dollars into her coffers, secure in the knowledge that, should the occasional torso-smearing Performance Artist manage to sneak through—no matter! "Our Kitty" will see to it that only the finest Swiss chocolate is used!

Some, it is said, are born elegant. Some achieve elegance. Some have elegance thrust upon them. The word itself, however, was invented by Kitty Carlisle Hart.

*New York City*       *1990*

# Douglas Fairbanks, Jr.
## BY
# Buddy Rogers

What can I say about Douglas Fairbanks, Jr.—Doug, Jr.—Let's see—first of all, we are related but just how neither of us can quite figure out! Since my late wife, Mary Pickford, was his stepmother—what am I? His stepfather once removed? He often signs his letters "Your stepson," (with a great big question mark)! One thing I am very sure of—we have been the best of friends for fifty years or more. Doug, Jr., visited Mary and me often at Pickfair. Mary and I were always so delighted to have him, and he was told to come often and to stay as long as he liked. In other words, Pickfair was his home also.

A short time ago, I was asked by Thames Television to fly to London for a surprise television show honoring Doug, Jr.—a *This Is Your Life* type program. He was really surprised to see me and even more surprised to learn I was wearing a suit made by a tailor he had sent me to in London in the late thirties! He was astounded to see that it still fit!

We have had so many good times over the years. He has a standing invitation to visit my new wife Beverly and me at Pickfair Lodge, a home I built and furnished with the furniture, paintings, and artifacts from the old Pickfair. The guest house looks the same as the one he stayed in for so many years at Pickfair.

Douglas Fairbanks, Jr., has always been a superb actor, truly a superstar, a great gentleman, a man of great wit, a humanitarian, and above all a true and loving friend. There is only one change that I can see over all these years and that is the title "Sir"—and I am so proud of my dear friend, Sir Douglas Fairbanks, Jr.

*New York City      1986*

# Derek Jacobi
## BY
# Kenneth Branagh

Having been asked to write something about Derek Jacobi, I have since spent many weeks agonizing over what to say.

It needs something witty and intelligent. Something that can convey his enormous talent, his kindness and humour.

The truth is, I find it impossible to do justice in my actor's would-be purple prose to this particular man.

To put it as simply as possible then.

Derek is one of the greatest actors I have ever seen. He has moved me to tears of joy and sadness through his work.

He is also one of the nicest people I know, a great friend and a wonderful companion round the dinner table. He has been as kind to me over the years as anyone I've met in the acting profession (and, by the way, he's also a great jiver).

He's all these things and many more which I feel unable to embarrass him with (he's a great blusher).

I just love him.

*Studio City, California        1984*

# Brooke Shields
## BY
# Charles Durning

I have known Brookie since she was 11 or 12, and I was pleasantly surprised to find how well adjusted she was to her fame because even at that age she was very well known worldwide.

Over the years, we have kept in touch and she is still the same wonderful, lovely, beautiful person I have always known, only more so now because she has become mature and has strong convictions about life. She has a loyalty and a kind of trusting innocence shared by few, but still has a shrewdness about her to know who are her friends and who are not.

I loved her at 11 and I love her now, but even more than that, I like her and trust her.

*Studio City, California*    *1992*

# John Mills
## BY
# John Candy

"Good actors are good because of the things they can tell us without talking. When they are talking, they are the servants of the dramatist. It is what they can show the audience when they are not talking that reveals the fine actor."

*Sir Cedric Hardwick*—1958

Sir Cedric may well have written this about Sir John Mills' Academy Award–winning performance in *Ryan's Daughter*.

Like millions of people around the world, I've been a fan of Sir John's work for many, many years. His characterizations never cease to amaze and entertain me. In fact, *Tunes of Glory* is a film I've actually worn out and had to replace. Moreover, as Lt. Col. Barrows, Sir John, in my humble opinion, gave the performance of a lifetime. It's no wonder Sir John Mills is recognized by his peers as one of the great actors of this century.

*Hollywood        1983*

# Johnny Mathis
## BY
# Dionne Warwick

In a word, SILK!

# Dorothy Jeakins
## BY
# Julie Andrews

My friend, Dottie Jeakins, writes marvelous letters. She forms a long, narrow column of words—sometimes a short, wide one—in the center of the page, then leaves a generous margin and fills every edge of her Narcissus-white paper with thoughts and afterthoughts, all written with a fine pen in the blackest ink. She adds a small drawing; a flower, a heart. The result is a gift, unique and clear, like Dottie herself.

She has designed the costumes for a host of films over the years—all of them enhanced by her personal vision. Her work is pure, radiant, with an absolute lack of fuss. She has an exceptional knowledge of period, shape, and cut, and combines details and textures with a superb, delicate sense of colour. She draws beautifully, and her creations are so utterly right that they make one feel sane.

She reminds me of those strong pioneer ladies who crossed the country in covered wagons. You notice her face first: the merry, dark eyes, the high brow, generous mouth, little make-up, simplicity of hair caught up by a bone comb or peasant scarf. She is quite tall, slim and big-boned—long legs, the whole giving an impression of grace. She wears marvelous fabrics, flat shoes, and there is always a subtle detail added—a brooch, a bangle, or some hand-painted buttons. She laughs like a young girl—shy and surprised when humour catches her unexpectedly.

I know little about her background, but one is aware that there may have been childhood pain, yet she exhibits courage and strength. She is fiercely private. There is nothing artificial about her: no guile. She infuses everything she does with a sense of dignity. She is a loyal friend, soft, caring. I find myself smiling as I write about her.

This portrait of Dottie captures her well. The baroque piece on the wall behind her suggests, better than my words ever could, the complicated passion that I suspect she carries inside, but that I'm sure few have glimpsed.

*Los Angeles*      *1965*

# Suzanne Pleshette
## BY
# Bob Newhart

It sure doesn't seem like 19 years ago, but it is. In the fall of 1971, we were in the process of casting the part of Emily for the pilot of *The Bob Newhart Show*. A lot of names of actresses, some big, some unknown, had been thrown around, but none that had MTM, the producers or myself all that excited.

Early, on a Thursday morning, I received a phone call from Arthur Price, my manager and one of the co-founders of MTM Productions. He said, "I've found your wife." "I didn't know she was missing," I replied. "No, idiot, your television wife." (We had developed a warm personal relationship over the years.) "I was watching the Carson show last night," he continued, "and Suzanne Pleshette was one of the guests. I think she would make a perfect Emily." I knew immediately he was right. Suzie would be perfect.

A meeting was set up between Suzie, myself, the producers, Dave Davis and Lorenzo Music, and MTM's Grant Tinker, Arthur Price and their casting department. The part of the wife was crucial to the success of the show. Emily and Bob were to be the "glue" that would hold the show together, two islands of sanity surrounded by a group of zanies: Bill Daily, Peter Bonerz, Marcia Wallace and Jack Riley.

We read a scene from the pilot where, unable to have our own children, we try to adopt a baby. It was a magical moment, the chemistry was right. Emily was a true woman of the seventies. She loved her husband, was supportive and respected him, while at the same time having a career of her own.

I am convinced the Emily and Bob relationship was a major reason for the success and durability of the show. Two adult, mature people who had respect for one another. The relationship had such an impact on the viewers, that 19 years later in the filming of the last episode of *Newhart* the bedroom set from *The Bob Newhart Show* received applause when it was revealed to the live audience in the studio.

*Washington, D.C.*        *1985*

# Lew Ayres
## BY
# Laraine Day

Lew Ayres is one of the most wonderful men I've ever worked with—talented, intelligent, very kind, true to himself. And he has the most marvelous sense of humor—funny, offbeat, charming.

# Barbara Walters
## BY
# Carl Bernstein

Over the years, I have given Barbara Walters a lot more thought than you might expect, beginning on an inauspicious note in 1974:

Bob Woodward and I, still surprisingly wet behind the ears, had just published *All the President's Men* and we were booked on the *Today* show: the first time either of us had ever been interviewed on television. Barbara was a pussycat—friendly, reassuring, no tough questions—until there were hardly thirty seconds left on air. "How much money are you going to make off all this?" she asked.

Five years later, I became Washington bureau chief of ABC News. My first week on the job I got a call from Barbara. Would I come to Blair House with her and assist in her interview of Anwar Sadat? In the car Barbara was frenetic, unsure of herself. We went over her questions, talked about shifting the order of a few. And then we were in Blair House, under the lights. My memory of that afternoon is of two truly galvanizing figures: Barbara Walters and Anwar Sadat, seated across from each other, his ankle-high boots sparkling, his back ramrod-straight, his quickness of mind stunning—and his deference to Barbara Walters somehow unsurprising. The sense he conveyed was of being with another head of state. Her transformation—rock-steady, self-assured as the cameras rolled, was complete.

Many years later, Barbara and I found ourselves together at a dinner party at which a variation of Charades was played. And again I was struck by that girlish uncertainty, an almost child-like lack of self-assurance . . . and the determination to win and to acquit herself brilliantly. The game was not played strictly for enjoyment.

She inspires tremendous ambivalence in people. Perhaps that is her real stature. She has probably had more to do with the profound changes in American journalism in the second half of the 20th century than any reporter. On this I pass no judgment.

Provocative, irresistible, dangerous—she does her job incredibly well. Let us praise God—and Barbara—that television journalism is no longer a man's business. Yes, she has done puff pieces—but even those hold a strange fascination, perhaps more for their take on Barbara than on her subject. And then there are the interviews that are part of our time, a video history of our epoch—revealing, in-depth, thoughtful, tough. Interviews that stand apart and are unassailable

*Bel Air, California      1988*

and which exist utterly on their own terms. Genre pieces. She is the only person with the audacity—in her twinky way—to ask the President of the United States and his wife if they sleep in the same bed. "Oh come on Barb, get off it," I often find myself saying—and then I learn something utterly surprising.

She is a perfectionist . . . I suspect her greatest fear is that we will judge her lightweight, less than brilliant . . . or that we will dislike her.

But she is no lightweight, and she is infinitely clever. She is totally herself, an American original. And it is impossible to dislike her. And there, I suspect, is the secret of her success and longevity and our affection.

❏

# Sydney Guilaroff
## BY
# Debbie Reynolds

Sydney Guilaroff is not a "Hair Stylist"—He is an artist, as much as any of the great heads of departments who directed the technical achievements departments at M.G.M. in the "Golden Era."

When directors, writers, art directors, cinematographers, etc., traveled to France and other locations for research and for authentic information—Sydney went for the same reasons— *Voilà. Camille, Marie Antoinette*, to mention a couple.

Sydney—a man unique in manner and talents—a man who holds himself with dignity.

He has never allowed his work to become commercialized. He always believed his work was his art, and was not for sale.

He is decent, trustworthy, thoughtful, kind.

There is no hair designer now, or ever, who will achieve what Sydney has accomplished in films.

His name and work are listed on over 400 of the Industry's greatest films.

M.G.M. took unknown talents in the 30s, 40s, and 50s Golden Era, and handed these "diamonds in the rough" over to the studio's creative heads.

Drama—singing—dancing—fashion—make-up and hair.

Among the designers of fashion at that time were Adrian, Irene, Walter Plunkett, Ory Kelly, Helen Rose, Edith Head—to name a few. Drama—Lillian Burns. Diction—Gertrude Fogeler. Make-up—Jack Dawn and William Tuttle. Sydney Guilaroff headed the hair creations. The Golden Era of Hollywood brought to the world the most beautiful talented stars with a lot of credit for their stardom due, in part, to their teachers and stylists. Sydney helped to create most of the legendary glamorous female stars.

As long as film survives, their image and fame survives—also to mention a few of "His Ladies": Greta Garbo, Greer Garson, Norma Shearer, Joan Crawford, Hedy Lamarr, Rosalind Russell, Myrna Loy, Katharine Hepburn, Lana Turner, Ava Gardner, Grace Kelly, Marilyn Monroe, Shirley MacLaine, Judy Garland, Elizabeth Taylor, Cyd Charisse, Ann Miller, June Allyson, Leslie Caron, Vera Ellen, Ann Blyth, Jane Powell, Pier Angeli, and many more.

He went full cycle from Jeanette MacDonald to Ann-Margret.

From Judy to Liza.

His talent and work not only beautified and glamorized the stars, but identified the characters being portrayed.

He is our Prince, our royalty in the hairstyling world of motion pictures.
He more importantly is our friend.

# Cary Elwes
## BY
# Rob Reiner

It's Hollywood, it's 1927, and talkies are the wave of the future. You are the head of a major motion picture studio, and you are thrilled because your number one star, Cary Elwes, not only has the all-important dashing good looks, but he can speak, and speak eloquently. If he doesn't age, you have a talent that will last well into the 21st century. Timeless.

*Studio City, California*     *1990*

# Linda Darnell
## BY
# Tab Hunter

LINDA

I first saw Linda Darnell in person at a polo match at the old Riviera Country Club. I was a starstruck kid in those days, and she was, as the movie magazines proclaimed her, "A raven-haired beauty of the silver screen." Overnight, she had become the leading lady to such Hollywood heavyweights as Tyrone Power and Henry Fonda, in films like *Blood and Sand, The Mark of Zorro, Chad Hanna, Brigham Young,* and *Daytime Wife.*

As a striking young beauty, Linda was a creation of the studio system. She was highly valued as an incredible adornment to the 20th Century Fox studios program of high-styled product. What a beauty! Her quality was genuinely sweet, and her manner was totally unaffected. In her last few years at her "home" studio, she proved that she had served her apprenticeship well, by turning in performances of amazing versatility, humor and bite, in films like *Fallen Angel, Everybody Does It, Unfaithfully Yours, Letter to Three Wives, No Way Out,* and *My Darling Clementine.*

In the early fifties . . . at the outward lip of her successes, I was fortunate enough to be the recipient of her encouragement and kindness. I was a nervous wreck during the screen test for my first starring role in a film called *Island of Desire.* "Relax," she said, "I'm good luck for beginners." She was just that. Linda played a major role in helping to launch my career and I will never forget her for it. She was incredible to me.

I often wondered about the fabric of her life over the next twelve years that passed, until her untimely death in that fire in Chicago in 1965. Professionally, she functioned most successfully at the major studio that made her a "star." Personally, she lingers on to all who ever knew her. I never knew her well . . . but I loved her.

*Phoenix, Arizona*     *1951*

# George Hurrell
## BY
# Loretta Young

As an actress, there is nothing more stimulating than knowing that you are working with experts. I learned from an older actor, many years ago, "The better your co-workers are, the better you look."

And when it comes to portrait photography, of all the gifted men and woman with whom I've been fortunate enough to work, there is no one better than George Hurrell. He is on a mountaintop all his own, and *has* been ever since I first met him more than fifty years ago.

I was about twenty-three at my first sitting with him, and seventy-six at my last; I can't begin to remember how many there were in between. I am delighted to say he is still the "Rembrandt" in the world of portrait photographers. Happily, his talent has grown right along with him.

I really do love George Hurrell: I love his sensitivity; I love his quietness; I love his lack of pretension; I love the ease with which he works; I love the music with which he chooses to work. Most of all, I love the continuing search for beauty in everything he sees and does.

I can't find the exact words to describe a George Hurrell portrait, but I always recognize one when I see it. How many times have we *all* said, "Oh yes, that's a Hurrell. Isn't he Great?!"

*Hollywood        1981*

# Robert Ryan
## BY
# Robert Wise

Robert Ryan was one of our outstanding character–leading man stars of the post–World War II period. For a director, he was a joy—sensitive, creative, inventive, adaptable, highly professional—all one could want in an actor.

As a private citizen, Robert Ryan was equally impressive. He was thoughtful, considerate, lively, fun, caring, very much involved with his fellow man. A life-long liberal, he was always concerned with people's welfare and spoke out and fought for the underdog all his life.

Knowing and working with Bob Ryan was one of the most stimulating and warm experiences of my many years of making films.

*New York City      1967*

# Twiggy Lawson
## BY
# Tony Walton

Who's prettier by far and a far brighter star than Miss Piggy? Well, Twiggy.

Who's forthright and fearless yet even more humble than Piglet? Our Twiglet.

Who makes you feel runny inside just like Syrup of Figs?* Sweet Twiggs.

Who somehow serenely combines both the solemn *and* sizzly? Just Lizzly . . .

I mean Leslie . . . Leslie Hornby . . . Lawson that is. See how just thinking about her makes a person discombobulated!

She first got me rattled when we worked together on the dizzying adventure of Ken Russell's version of *The Boy Friend*, her enchanting debut as an actress, singer, dancer after her "swinging 60's" years as the most ubiquitous, the most original and certainly the most adorable clothes-horse ever to grace the pages of every imaginable magazine worldwide.

Later, after her triumph on Broadway in *My One and Only*, she appeared with Tommy Tune on the British Royal Variety Show, doing their delightfully demented water dance. In introducing them, Laurence Olivier said something like: "If a young cockney lass from Neasden asks, 'How do I get to Broadway?' she'd invariably be told, 'You can't get there from here.'" Yet this amazingly gutsy and entirely golden-hearted creature made that apparently impossible trip with ease—and, to general astonishment, immediately won the hard heart of Broadway.

She was—as Olivier also said—magical.

But, typically, so much of this special magic seems to be carefully reserved for friends and family. For her enchanted daughter Carly, who—from a very early age—could amaze you with her detailed drawings of any number of classic cartoon characters. And for her boisterously

*The English kids' equivalent of Castor Oil.

*Studio City, California*     *1992*

gifted and loving Leigh—who wooed and ultimately wed her under our Sag Harbor willow tree in a never to be forgotten ceremony.

In proposing to her a few days earlier, Leigh had asked if she'd like to be married at Sag and she'd replied in that never entirely abandoned Cockney, "Why do we 'ave to be married at the Screen Actors Guild?"

Ah Twiggs—don't change a hair for us, not if you care for us. And how could we not care—forever—for her? She is a one-of-a-kind . . . and still barely mined . . . Treasure.

◻

# Burton Lane
## BY
# Sheldon Harnick

Melody . . .
pure, fresh streams
   of melody . . .
Melodies that
   soar and strut . . .
Melodies that
   smile and sigh . . .
Melodies that
   caress and exhilarate . . .
Melting melodies that
   float, dance and glide . . .

Fountains of melody . . .
   playful, rich . . .
      graceful, tender . . .
Glowing gifts
   from the singing heart
      of Burton Lane.

*New York City*      *1990*

# James Coco
## BY
# Doris Roberts

When you just think of JIMMY COCO, it brings a smile to your lips. Jimmy my pal, my mentor, my acting partner, my gambling partner, my dining out partner, my diet partner, was the most outrageously funny, sweetest, dearest, generous, nourishing, affectionate friend I've ever known and one of the best things that ever happened in my life.

"Life is not a dress rehearsal, Doris, this is it!" he would remind me on occasion.

Jimmy possessed an abundance of love and he was blessed with a generosity of spirit, not only for his friends but for all of his colleagues.

Whenever I had a disappointment, either in my career or everyday living, Jimmy was always there for me. "Turn it around, Honey, turn it around," and in no time he had me screaming with laughter.

*Joy*, according to the dictionary, is to experience great pleasure or delight. He certainly gave us that.

All his friends were his lovers.

The last thing Jimmy ever said to me was, "You and I have been lovers all these years, we just never fooled around."

Once I asked him what theatre meant to him. "I love to make people laugh, it's an enormous high. I love leaving the theatre feeling good, and if I can make people feel like that, I think that's wonderful."

What a legacy to leave.

Thanks, Jimmy. Thank you, my friend.

*Los Angeles        1982*

# Vanessa Redgrave
## BY
# Peter Hall

Vanessa Redgrave's acting is the embodiment of truth; and it looks easy. But we must qualify this. We praise an actor's performance because it has "truth"; but the word cannot be an accurate description of acting, because *acting* is always a pretense, a lie. Paradoxically, it is the sincerity of the actor's art, his commitment to the lie, if you like, which makes his "truth."

Vanessa is complete in her communication. In the theatre, she speaks from the heart; on the screen, the camera seems to see right into her being. The audience knows what she is thinking. There is apparently no art, no artifice: only "truth." It is clear, like a crystal.

Vanessa lives as she acts, by deep conviction. I don't always agree with her opinions, but I always agree with her art. And I believe both must be heard.

She has been called the greatest actress in the English-speaking world. While I don't believe there is a greatest or a best, I know from happy experience that she belongs with the greatest actors I have worked with—with Olivier, Laughton, Richardson, Gielgud, Scofield, Ashcroft . . . They all share in rehearsal an ability to become somebody else instantaneously and completely. From a standing start they create an incandescent moment of truth. It always shocks me that they can immediately return to themselves and comment—sometimes critically—on what they have just created. In all honesty, they make truth out of a world of pretense. So whenever she acts, Vanessa helps me understand myself and my fellows a little more.

*Hollywood     1990*

# Michael Hordern
## BY
# Diana Rigg

I was first in a play with Michael Hordern in 1962, *The Physicists* by Dürrenmatt, directed by Peter Brook for the R.S.C. I don't remember him very well. We had no scenes together, which was just as well since I was rather bad as a plodding Teutonic nurse. Ten years passed during which Michael played many leading Shakespearean roles and starred in several West End successes. It wasn't until 1972, when we were both cast in Tom Stoppard's *Jumpers* at The National, that I was able to watch this consummate actor work from close quarters. For Michael, it was that God-given moment when the part of a lifetime comes alive. He seized it and his interpretation will, I predict, always be remembered as definitive. Not that it was easy. As George, a metaphysician, Michael had lengthy and fiendishly difficult speeches. The play was long and physically taxing, but he triumphed. He did so with an exquisite balance of intellect and endearing eccentricity. Like Richardson and Guinness, he is a particularly English actor. He represents to the public the marriage of two qualities that make our theatre great: tradition and individualism.

# Doris Day
## BY
# James Stewart

I did one picture with Doris Day, *The Man Who Knew Too Much*. We did it in Marrakesh, Morocco.

Doris did a wonderful job throughout the picture and Alfred Hitchcock was very pleased with her work. They got along fine.

Doris came into the picture with a song, "Que Sera, Sera." I don't think Hitchcock was very familiar with songs in his pictures and he wasn't sure of this one. As it turned out, the song was just as big a hit as the picture, maybe bigger.

Doris was something very special and Hitchcock, and all of us, enjoyed doing the picture with her.

*Universal City, California      1960*

# Truman Capote
## BY
# Lauren Bacall

During the making of *Beat the Devil*, Bogie said of Truman—"At first you don't believe he's real—then after awhile you want to put him in your pocket and take him home with you"—He also said he had never seen anyone work as hard as Truman did. An unlikely pair—they remained good friends.

To me he meant fun, intelligence, originality and finally, loneliness and sadness. He was a plus—someone I looked forward to.

His gift was with his pen and I will always be grateful for that, and for his friendship.

*New York City* 1960

# Walter Matthau
## BY
# Carol Matthau

Walter Matthau is a series of counterpoints. Many people are—but, usually, on the down side. His goes up to the sky. The adjectives that I read in some of his movie reviews really don't seem to describe him in any recognizable way, but I am leaving out his greatness as an actor. His duality is romantic, tender, loving, aesthetic—most tasteful—innate elegance—deeply good manners—and with a compassion that goes all the way around the world. He has every kind of generosity—money is just a starting point. Does he have any faults?   No.   He's perfect.

*Pacific Palisades, California*       *1990*

# Jean Simmons
## BY
# Deborah Kerr

What an exquisite face, and what a dear, funny person! We worked together for the first time in *Black Narcissus*, and with her dusky make-up she looked even more beautiful as the Indian seductress! We have been friends ever since, even though I don't often see her.

On *The Grass Is Greener* (in which she played the zany girlfriend of Cary Grant), she was quite enchanting and hilariously funny, and we started talking in Cockney accents and, like two schoolgirls, couldn't stop! What fun we had. A lovely actress and a lovely person. I only wish I saw her more often.

*Holmby Hills, California      1964*

# Kenneth Branagh
## BY
# Andy Garcia

As actors we are in constant search for good material, for inspiration. As Kenneth looks toward Shakespeare at times for this, I will follow his example and turn toward José Martí, poet, patriot and hero of Cuba's struggle for independence against Spain:

> I'll cultivate a white rose
> in June or in January
> for a sincere man
> who gives me his
> honest hand.

Kenneth is a hard act to follow, but I would follow him anywhere.

*Studio City, California*      *1991*

# Peggy Ann Garner
## BY
# Piper Laurie

I thought we looked so much alike when we were eleven.

Some long lost sister. My closest friend.

I wept with her (and me) on the roof in Brooklyn.

I shared her pain.

Sometimes I even thought I was her.

Years later when we were both grown, we actually met briefly in a New York rehearsal hall.

I was unable to tell her how touched I had been by her artistry.

Debut, *St. Louis, Missouri*      *1953*
*New York City*      *1959*   (page 138)

# Harrison Ford
## BY
# Jessica Tandy

I have never worked with Harrison Ford and know him only enough to say "How do you do" to him on various occasions.

But I have a deep admiration for him as an actor.

I know when I see him on the big screen that I will see a performance of truth, energy, and consummate skill and I leave the theatre filled with admiration.

His body of work already is impressive, and he will have a long and rewarding career. He's a stayer.

*Brentwood, California       1991*

# Clifford Odets
## BY
# Luise Rainer

Clifford. There was so much strength in him, so much tenderness, so much violence, but even when storming and often destroying there always was that aching for love. Music was what stilled him. He listened intently, he needed it, and it nourished him. It seemed to make him reach out and up as though to try and scratch the blue from the sky to see behind it the unseen. Within his wild inextricable maze he was always lovable.

*Beverly Hills*        *1957*

# Geraldine Fitzgerald
## BY
# Sidney Lumet

She comes bouncing into a room, and I mean bouncing. There is a rapid rise and fall to her. Her hand reaches out and takes yours and a smile appears on her face so that you think the sun is rising. The room has changed. Geraldine Fitzgerald has arrived.

She is incandescent. All the time. Even when she's nervous. Even when she's struggling to find the truth of the part. It is not surprising that Bernard Shaw is one of her heroes. I believe he coined the phrase "life force," and that's Geraldine. Giving, loving, spreading joy and inspiration. She is a very serious angel.

*New York City*     *1956*

# Walter Wanger
## BY
# Irene Sharaff

Walter thoroughly enjoyed being a producer and he was a very good producer: sensitive, sensible, patient. Elegant, he had taste and tact—plus a fine sense of humor, often wryly directed at himself. Among his many productions the material he chose was often more interesting and pertinent to the times than most of the films of that period. He secured the rights for Lawrence Durrell's *The Alexandria Quartet* long before it became a best-seller, the fourth volume in fact still in typescript. It was sad he did not live to see it made into a film.

*Rome, Italy*      *1961*

# Morgan Fairchild
## BY
# C. Everett Koop, M.D.

We use the term "gun barrel vision" in medicine to describe the view of a situation or event as though seeing it only through a long pipe—narrowly focused, devoid of background—a gun barrel. That's how I first saw Morgan Fairchild.

Of course I knew of her, had caught fleeting glimpses on television of an unusual face, a striking figure, the sense that to know more of her would promise uniqueness.

In the early days of the mystery, confusion, fear, and prejudice of AIDS when my life was governed more by pressure than by choice, I found myself having breakfast with Morgan Fairchild at the Beverly Hilton. What a genuine person. I suppose I had expected some facade, something artificial, even some personal aggrandizement. But, no, she was making herself available as a spokesperson to young people about the facts and myths about AIDS—advice they were more likely to take from a beautiful role model than a bearded septuagenarian. And so our too brief and too sporadic friendship began.

About a year later I was to be honored at a large Washington gathering for my efforts to educate Americans about AIDS. Barbara Bush was to make the presentation. Without my knowledge she had to cancel. It was Morgan Fairchild who hopped on a plane in Los Angeles and flew to Washington just to present me with my award and her thanks. I don't know who asked her to come. I know she didn't have to—it was a call beyond any conceivable obligation. But she came. I will never forget it and cherish the moment to this day.

Morgan Fairchild should never be seen with gun barrel vision. Only a wide-angle lens does her justice. Beautiful—outside and in.

*Long Beach, California*        *1979*

# Dick Smith
## BY
# Hal Holbrook

Dick Smith is the pattern of dynamic energy contained by patience. His artistry springs out of this control, this tautness of intelligence and sensitivity. Amusement, modesty, and awareness of what is true quietly attend his great skill.

One incident captures Dick Smith in action. In 1967 he devised the make-up for a television special of *Mark Twain Tonight!* The hairpieces were made in Bob Kelly's New York shop. Dick was shaping the Twain eyebrows with a tweezer one night when Kelly looked up, saying: "Just pull the door shut when you're finished, Dick." Kelly went to dinner and a show. When he returned four hours later to get something he'd forgotten, Dick was still working on the eyebrows.

*Universal City, California*     *1990*

# Michael Feinstein
## BY
# Jule Styne

Michael Feinstein is a rare treat to our musical world.

His phrasing of lyrics would have pleased Larry Hart, Ira Gershwin, Cole Porter, Frank Loesser—in fact all lyric writers love his understanding of a lyric.

Wait till you hear our album.

# Hermes Pan
## BY
# Ginger Rogers

Hermes Pan—one of the most clever of those people titled "choreographer."

Webster's dictionary says:
"Hermes—ancient Greek god of the wood or shepherds. A deity, the son of Zeus and Maya. The messenger of the gods . . . and many of the arts of life. Commonly figured as a youth with a rod, a brimmed hat and winged shoes."

"Pan—to fit or join together."

Hermes was really blessed with the ability to join Fred Astaire and me in all ten of the musical films we made together.

So, the song title, "Shoes With Wings On" from *The Barkleys of Broadway* was a typical Fred and Hermes number. A most outstanding act of joining the dancing individual to his music.

Hermes Pan had a shy personality, but was a warm and friendly man with a soft voice and ready humor.

They just don't make them like him anymore!!

*Beverly Hills*          *1990*

# Lee Grant
## BY
# Michael Douglas

It's as if she's listening to you with her eyes. Lee sees what you are trying to say. Her sage-like nod, followed by a slight Cheshire smile, makes you feel so secure . . . or uncertain, depending on how truthful your thoughts are.

I don't think I've ever met anybody with a greater sense of honesty than Lee. Professionally, it's a talent she cultivates. As a teacher, actress, and director, her work has inspired her students, co-stars, and cast to give the best performances of their careers.

Personally, she can't help but bring the best out of everybody. Her truth has caused her great pain during strange political times in this country, and tremendous joy amongst the company of her daughters, husband, and friends.

It's that silent rage in her eyes; she's taught me to listen by looking. The ability to turn the emotion of anger into a demand for truth, and succeed—that's inspirational.

*Los Angeles        1980*

# Maurice Evans
## BY
# Helen Hayes

To write about Maurice Evans gives me pleasure because it requires me to think about him in depth. That is indeed a healing use of a mind overcrowded with too many memories of too many people, too many happenings.

His gifts to me have been his performances first off, and after those I have enjoyed his fun. I do miss laughing with Maurice—even sometimes *at* Maurice. Like the times he assumed his Colonel Blimp role and told off the peasants: "No, I will *not* order your seven course dinner—I will *not* be force-fed!" This to a startled innkeeper in the heart of Romania. I laughed my way with him over a large portion of the globe, but mostly I have missed his guidance on the boards. His taste was impeccable, his generosity, at least with me, was boundless.

Twenty-some years ago Maurice lured me from retirement to join him in a bus and truck tour of the United States. We played chapels, schools, town halls, and at least one football stadium. As we stood at the very top of the auditorium to look down at our playing space, I took fright. "I'm going to roll on that stage in my green dress looking like a pickle." Maurice, the confirmed bachelor, gave me a long look and said quite seriously, "You know, I often think I should have changed the habits of a lifetime and asked you to marry me."

Thank you, Maurice.

*Los Angeles*    *1980*

# Dorothy McGuire
## BY
# Robert Young

To me Dorothy is a consummate artist. This was proven beyond the shadow of a doubt when we worked together in *The Enchanted Cottage*. It was intended to change her appearance to create a contrast with how she appears to her lover. She refused, saying, "I'll play her plain and unattractive and forlorn." And she did. I can't think of another actress who would not respond, "You must put on lots of makeup to make me look ugly."

# Walter Pidgeon
## BY
# Greer Garson

Someone once said about Walter:

"A man's man—

A woman's dream."

*Bel Air, California*      *1979*

# David Hockney
## BY
# Helmut Newton

He is the most innovative and stimulating of artists and never ceases to amaze me with his use of technology and whatever comes his way to produce art. He takes anything from technology and bends and twists it to produce his very own works of art. During my preoccupation with swimming pools, I always wished I could photograph like he painted.

*Los Angeles*      *1988*

# Elizabeth Taylor
## BY
# Charles Champlin

Once upon another time in another place, I spent a little while talking with Elizabeth Taylor. It was just after *Cleopatra* finished shooting and she was more than usually in the center of the world's attention. I thought then, and think now, that she bears the burden of celebrity with wonderful and unaffected ease. She was warm, natural, wise, spontaneous, funny and, on that distant London afternoon, supremely happy.

Celebrity, for all it is sought after by those who lack it, can be curiously isolating and difficult. Elizabeth Taylor is so famous for being Elizabeth Taylor that it has become too easy to forget—I mean for producers and studio executives to forget—that she is a very, very good actress. It is not enough that she should be selling perfume and valiantly raising money for AIDS research; she should be engaged again as an actress, doing material worthy of her gifts, her beauty, and her experience in her craft. Celebrity didn't create Martha in *Who's Afraid of Virginia Woolf?;* Elizabeth Taylor did, with due credit to Edward Albee and Mike Nichols. And I hope she will be granted the opportunity to extend the remarkable gallery of characterizations she began when she was not yet in her teens. Being famous is nice, but it is not enough.

*Bel Air, California*       *1991*   (page 169)
*Puerto Vallarta, Mexico*       *1964*
(Doodles on contact sheet by Elizabeth Taylor)

# Lee J. Cobb
## BY
# Arthur Miller

As rehearsals proceeded for *Death of a Salesman* in the small, periodically abandoned theatre on the ratty roof of the New Amsterdam on Forty-second Street, where Ziegfeld in the twenties had staged some intimate revues, Lee seemed to move about in a buffalo's stupefied trance, muttering his lines, plodding with deathly slowness from position to position, and behaving like a man who had been punched in the head. "He's just learning it," Kazan shakily reassured me after three or four days. I waited as a week went by, and then ten days, and all that was emerging from Lee Cobb's throat was a bumpy hum. The other actors were nearing performance levels, but when they had to get a response from Lee all their rhythms slowed to near collapse. Kazan was no longer so sure and kept huddling with Lee, trying to pump him up. Nor did Lee offer any explanation, and I wondered whether he thought to actually play the part like a man with a foot in the grave. Between us, Kazan and I began referring to him as "the Walrus."

On about the twelfth day, in the afternoon, with Eddie Kook, our lighting supplier, and Jimmy Proctor, our pressman, and Kazan and myself in the seats, Lee stood up as usual from the bedroom chair and turned to Mildred Dunnock and bawled, "No, there's more people now . . . There's more people!" and, gesturing toward the empty upstage where the window was supposed to be, caused a block of apartment houses to spring up in my brain, and the air became sour with the smell of kitchens where once there had been only the odors of earth, and he began to move frighteningly, with such ominous reality that my chest felt pressed down by an immense weight. After the scene had gone on for a few minutes, I glanced around to see if the others had my reaction. Jim Proctor had his head bent into his hands and was weeping, Eddie Kook was looking shocked, almost appalled, and tears were pouring over his cheeks, and Kazan behind me was grinning like a fiend, gripping his temples with both hands, and we knew we had it—there was an unmistakable wave of life moving across the air of the empty theatre, a wave of Willy's pain and protest. I began to weep myself at some point that was not particularly sad, but it was as much, I think, out of pride in our art, in Lee's magical capacity to imagine, to collect within himself every mote of life since Genesis and to let it pour forth. He stood up there like a giant moving the Rocky Mountains into position.

At the end of the act, Del Hughes, our sweet but hardheaded, absolutely devoted, competent stage manager, came out from a wing and looked out at us. His stunned eyes started us all laughing. I ran up and kissed Lee, who pretended to be surprised. "But what did you expect, Arthur?" he said, his eyes full of his playful vanity. My God, I thought—he really *is* Willy! On the subway going home to Brooklyn I felt once again the aching pain in my muscles that the performance had tensed up so tightly, just as in the writing time. And when I thought of it later, it seemed as though Lee's sniffing around the role for so long recapitulated what I had done in the months before daring to begin to write.

*New York City*      1956

# Gene Hackman
## BY
# Arthur Penn

HACKMAN, GENE, U.S. Marine at sixteen, tender to the touch. His feelings, fierce and gentle, he dares show to all: this private man. He rages, and returns to the pain of the day with grace and works hard. He performs our comedy, searingly. A noble man, whose modesty in the face of fame amazes. A great actor, my friend Hackman is.

*Culver City, California*     *1990*

# Farley Granger
## BY
# Joan Collins

I first saw Farley Granger in a movie magazine called *Picturegoer* when I was a schoolgirl in London. I thought he had the most beautiful male face I had ever seen. I cut out his picture and pasted it on my desk, gazing at it admiringly when lessons became more than tedious.

In Hollywood, a few years later, I was cast as Evelyn Nesbit in *The Girl in the Red Velvet Swing* at 20th Century Fox. When I was informed that my first leading man was to be Farley Granger, my girlish excitement was barely containable.

I was petrified with nerves and excitement the day of our first rehearsals, but when Farley strolled in and chatted to me in the joshing humorous way that was his trademark, it put me immediately at ease, for he turned out to be just as beautiful as a person as he was physically. And he still is!

*New York City      1956*

# Shirley Booth
## BY
# Julie Harris

Who was Shirley?   What was she?   Well, a genius for one, a lovable lady for another, with a wicked sense of humor, and a good and loving neighbor for still another. When I moved to Cape Cod, Massachusetts in the late 1970's I called on Shirley Booth Baker in her home in North Chatham to say I was now her neighbor and that I had always adored her. After that, she called me to ask me if I would like to pick fresh peas in a friend's garden, and from then on our friendship bloomed. I have listened, enthralled, to her talk about her early days in the theatre, in stock companies, on the popular radio show written by her first husband, "Duffy's Tavern"— her voice was enchanting and so funny, then acting with Miss Hepburn in Barry's "The Philadelphia Story," and then coming into her own—a star for all of us, in "Come Back, Little Sheba" by William Inge—and "Sheba" seems to be the favorite. I loved Shirley for so many things, her impeccable timing, her truth, her great wit and simplicity. She was the consummate actress of stage, screen, and television. She has conquered them all and I smiled when I saw her Oscar, won in 1952 for her Lola in "Come Back, Little Sheba," sitting on the window sill of her sun room with the cord of the sun screen wrapped around it—Oscar holding up Shirley's window shade—a practical use for Mrs. Baker's prize.

I have heard Shirley say—"I love the stage best of all. I love to feel the audience there." Oh, Shirley and we were so lucky to have you in a theatre—on a stage.

Three cheers for you, Shirley Booth Baker.

I love you.

*Los Angeles*          *1963*

**177**

# Sir Lew Grade
## BY
# Shirley MacLaine

*(Hold up to a mirror to read)*

Love & luck to a heart
as big as his ego.
When I look at him
in a mirror it makes
me laugh.
He is a original
treasure and "Love" one
& Ralph!

*Beverly Hills    1990*

# Helmut Newton

## BY

# Dennis Hopper

Dear Helmut,

Rarely in my life have I looked at contemporary paintings and photographs and known that they would be around for the long haul. Eternity. My feeling is that an artist, at best, cheats death by leaving something that exists beyond his own lifetime. I knew immediately upon seeing your work and your individual stamp that I could separate a Helmut Newton photograph from all others. I am quite envious and jealous, not only of your great photographic message, but I would like to meet and know most of your subjects intimately.

*White Women* is one of the best photographic books of this century. I have to compare it to Henri Cartier-Bresson's *The Decisive Moment* and Robert Frank's *America*. It had that kind of impact on me. And since photography is little more than 100 years old, that's pretty impressive.

You are one of the nicest, kindest people, and you are truly where the word gentleman comes from. All my salutations to you and that other wonderful photographer in your family, Alice Springs.

And to quote from Joyce Cary, *The Horse's Mouth*, "You're one of them, Mr. Jamison. You're a Michelangelo, a Da Vinci, a Raphael."

Much love,
Your friend and admirer,

*West Hollywood*        *1992*

# Nancy Carroll
## BY
# Barry Paris

Something in the black-and-white pictures—moving and still alike—tells you Nancy Carroll's hair was bright red. Those big, bright Irish eyes had color, too. "I want drapes of a special shade of blue," Ethel Barrymore once commanded her decorator, "—the blue of Nancy Carroll's eyes."

Carroll's colors were conveyed on screen and confirmed off: A pert and perky petrel, she was petulant and pesky, too, as Paramount would find out. Arguably the first star "made" by talkies, she got more fan mail than anyone else at her studio in 1930, which was ironic. When she arrived in 1927, Paramount thought it was getting just a pretty Broadway chorine, mercifully rechristened from the original Ann Veronica LaHiff. Not much was expected of her beyond dancing and keeping up her ingenue's good looks. But when Dorothy Arzner deftly directed her in the sudsy melodrama *Manhattan Cocktail* (1928), Paramount saw star potential for her as a serious dramatic actress, as well.

Just prior to that, she'd been given the lead in *Abie's Irish Rose*, a film of the ethnic-cornpone stage hit about an Irish bride and Jewish groom. (The more the critics trashed it, the longer it ran.) Paramount paid an unprecedented $500,000 for screen rights and teamed spunky Carroll with dreamy Buddy Rogers for the first of four times. But now the frightening miracle of talkies raised the Big Question: could she make it with a mike?

The answer was yes, in *The Shopworn Angel* (1929). Carroll was a tough-as-nails showgirl opposite Gary Cooper's starry-eyed soldier, and she even got a chance to sing ("A Precious Little Thing Called Love") at the end. Sound showed her singing to good, and her acting to better, advantage. But she was soon complaining about the quality of her scripts (*The Wolf of Wall Street*, for example). Either her *kvetching* or her good luck led to *The Devil's Holiday* (1930), in which she played a gold-digging manicurist transformed by love. Director Edmund Goulding had written the part for Jeanne Eagels, recent victim of a heroin overdose. Carroll took the part and ran with it to the Oscars, where she came in a close second to Norma Shearer (for *The Divorcée*)—in the days when they revealed the runner-up votes.

She was brilliant, too, as the unfaithful wife of a dull millionaire in Harry d'Arrast's *Laughter* (1930). This chic romantic comedy still has staying power, and so did Nancy Carroll through 1932, the year she made her most offbeat picture, *The Man I Killed*. Directed by Ernst Lubitsch, it was a thoughtful anti-war story—and a box-office disaster.

That rare Lubitsch flop was a bad omen: he never made another drama, and Nancy Carroll never made another movie worthy of her. High-tempered by nature, she became so openly critical of her screenplays that a new set of studio bosses spitefully dropped her when her contract expired in 1933. Her popularity was waning by then, anyway, and Carroll wasn't about to hang around long to watch it wane. She quit films forever in 1938.

But she never stopped working—in theater and later TV. She longed for a key character role in Hitchcock's *Torn Curtain* (1964), but it went to Lila Kedrova instead (and won her an Oscar). Undaunted, Carroll returned to the road show touring circuit and was starring with Bert Lahr in *Never Too Late* up to the very day of her death in 1965.

She was vivacious, hard-drinking and assertive to the end, as her good friend John Springer, the film publicist, attests. In the 1950s, when Springer decided to marry, the Catholic church rigidly refused its permission unless June, his Episcopalian bride-to-be, took six months of Roman Catholic instructions. There were absolutely "no exceptions," and so Springer sadly made plans for a service with a Justice of the Peace. But when Nancy Carroll found out about it, she was outraged. True to her temperament, she went straight to her friend Cardinal Spellman to chastise him for driving a boy and his bride away from the Church and to demand corrective action.

The Springers were married in a lovely Catholic ceremony at St. Patrick's Cathedral.

# Ricardo Montalban
## BY
# Christopher Hewett

In Spanish, *hidalgo* means a person of nobility. Ricardo Montalban is a true *hidalgo*. When I joined him as Lawrence in *Fantasy Island*—replacing Hervé Villechaize ("Tattoo"), no mean feat for a person of my size—I discovered Ricardo to be a helpful and generous actor, and a warm and caring friend. His wonderful humour helped me through my uneasy moments, in what was to be the beginning of my life in T.V. Series-Land.

*Los Angeles     1980*

# Marge and Gower Champion
## BY
# George Sidney

**SCHULTZ 'N' SCHULTZ***

True royalty of show business—perfection was their credo—doing the strut or keeping up with a herd of pachyderms, they gave their all, plus . . . Good enough was never good enough. I encouraged Gower to look through the camera—and gave him his first directorial assignment in a television show for the D.G.A. He was on his way. He gave us great and unique entertainment. The Champs will always be remembered as a *"class act"* on and off . . .


*characters they played in M.G.M.'s George Sidney version of *Showboat*.

# Van Johnson
## BY
## Stanley Donen

I first met Van Johnson when he and I were in the original production of *Pal Joey*.

He had a small role (I had an even smaller one), but every moment he was on stage he made interesting.

Van is what in sports is called "a Natural." Like Joe DiMaggio or Joe Louis. And like the two Joe's that "Naturalness" came from a combination of innate talent, and the endless refining of his craft.

He's wonderful to watch because he makes it look so easy.

*New York City*     *1990*

# Kathy Bates
## BY
# Fannie Flagg

Now this is the face of a woman.

In those eyes I see sister, daughter, mother, wife, teacher and friend. This is a beautiful face.

*Studio City, California*      *1992*

# Kenneth Tynan
## BY
# Joan Plowright

His full name was Kenneth Peacock Tynan and that middle name couldn't have been more appropriate.

As a celebrated undergraduate at Oxford he decked himself out in purple doe-skin suits, embroidered waistcoats, and voluminous opera cloaks, and made it his business to forget that he had been born illegitimately to a provincial pair in Birmingham.

He floated down to London where, like Oscar Wilde, whom he greatly admired, "he showed off, he disdained prudence, he delighted others and he delighted himself."

He also irritated a lot of others, provoked and encouraged them, laid himself wide open to their mockery, and died much too soon.

I miss him, as do the many in our profession who grew up with him, and who forgave him his excesses and were grateful for his passion and panache.

The theatre was news when Tynan was on *The Observer*; he made it hit the headlines because he wanted them for himself; he had as great a longing for the limelight as the Three Sisters had for Moscow.

He would have liked to have been a great actor or director, or perhaps a famous bullfighter or Ché Guevara. Instead he made his name by writing about them with a brilliance and flair unmatched by his contemporaries.

It was his own practical experience in theatre which gave his criticism such authority and importance; and his own particular touch of genius which gave it such style.

When he was gone even his enemies approved his epitaph: "The greatest English drama critic since George Bernard Shaw."

Ken, I think, could have done without the Bernard Shaw bit.

*Beverly Hills*      *1979*

# Donald O'Connor
## BY
# Phyllis Newman

When I first saw Donald O'Connor knock himself (and me) out performing "Make 'Em Laugh" in the movie *Singin' in the Rain*, I didn't know that someday I was going to marry the author of that film, or that many years later I would co-star with Mr. O'Connor in an original television musical. Even if I *had* been psychic, I couldn't have been more impressed with his talent, humor, charm and enormous appeal.

The show, *Olympus 7-0000*, was a musical mix of mythology and football written by Richard Adler. Donald played Hermes, messenger of the gods, and I played Mary, earthbound cutie who prays to the gods for her boyfriend's team to win.

As always, Donald was an attractive, eternally boyish clown who danced precisely, yet effortlessly, and sang in that wonderfully musical, rhythmic way that only certain dancers can. He was disciplined, courtly, generous. He never took himself too seriously . . . but his audiences do.

He's an irresistible American talent.

# Cheryl Crawford
## BY
# Sidney Kingsley

Roddy McDowall notes that his photo of Cheryl Crawford is the only one he remembers in which she is smiling and relaxed.

I told him that when I met Cheryl in the early days of the Group Theatre, she had very little to smile about and no time to relax.

Cheryl was one of the three directors of the Group Theatre. She would have loved to direct plays, but that was not her job; her job was to handle the unglamorous chores—raise money, negotiate with theatres and unions, and hardest of all, keep the Group actors, whom she lovingly called "this gang of wild-eyed fanatics," from imploding and evaporating the Group Theatre.

Cheryl adored Lee Strasberg and was convinced that his inspiration and his dream would build the Group Theatre into a quintessential part of the history of the American theatre—more, of the world theatre. I agreed with her. I was also convinced that, without Cheryl's management, the Group would have never achieved the eminence it did under Lee Strasberg's direction.

At the 50th anniversary of *Men in White* winning the Pulitzer Prize, New York University honored the occasion by presenting the play with student actors at the University theatre. It was a distinguished and beautiful production. Cheryl was deeply moved by it, and so was I, evoking as it did memories which I regard as the most treasured of my life.

Slightly diminished, however, on that occasion, when Cheryl told us that, having discovered my play, she passionately loved it and wanted the Group Theatre to produce it. However, many of the actors of the Group were devout Marxists and would only do a play that expressed their political beliefs. My play did not serve that purpose, so they wanted to reject it.

Cheryl then informed Lee and Harold Clurman, the other two directors, that if the Group Theatre did not produce the play, she was going to produce it herself with Theresa Helburn, the distinguished executive director of the Theatre Guild.

The next day Lee Strasberg met with the actors and addressed them, thus: "Many of you have asked me what this play has in common with you. I'll tell you. It is a play about idealism and you are all, each in your own way, idealists. That is why you are here. That is why I am here. It is what the Group Theatre is about. That is the dream that we are working towards. So, if you have no further objection, we'll start rehearsing the play tomorrow."

*New York City        1956*

When Lee spoke about the theatre, he had the fervor of a prophet of the Old Testament. Cheryl loved him for that. So did all the others. He was the spiritual force that held this Group of rugged individualists together; and when the actors rebelled against Lee's authority, Cheryl was horrified and resigned from the Group Theatre. The next day, Lee resigned. Without Lee and Cheryl, the Group fluttered along but soon it withered and died.

But this was a dream that did not die easily, and Cheryl was determined that it would not die. She enlisted Bobby Lewis and Elia Kazan and together they formed the Actors Studio, which in essence was one way to preserve the inheritance of the old dream.

But Cheryl was now a successful producer on her own; Bobby Lewis was a successful teacher and director; and Elia Kazan was perhaps the most coveted director in the American Theatre and in films. They were much too busy on their own projects to hold the Studio together. A year later, Bobby Lewis resigned. Cheryl now felt that the Studio was doomed unless . . . but she wasn't going to let that happen.

She persuaded Lee Strasberg to lecture at the Actors Studio. When Lee spoke about the theatre, he was irresistible and Cheryl knew it. The actors were deeply moved. Cheryl was exultant. Triumphant, she told me, "Wasn't Lee magnificent? Now he's going to take over the Actors Studio. We've saved it. When Lee talked, I was so excited," she murmured, "I peed in my pants," and she smiled that mischievous smile which Cheryl very rarely indulged in. Examine Roddy McDowall's photo closely. That is the way Cheryl looked at that triumphant moment; that is the way I like to remember her.

Cheryl was right; Lee did indeed take over the Actors Studio and was the inspiring force that made its actors the inheritors of the dream of the Group Theatre. Cheryl had done it again.

Lee never let go, even in death; symbolically he seemed reluctant to let the Actors Studio go. His funeral cortege on the way to the cemetery slowly moved down to the Actors Studio where it paused outside for ten minutes. The actors, many of them at the courtyard of the Studio, wept. Finally Lee and the hearse went on . . . Reluctantly! Very reluctantly, for the cortege turned around the corner and came back again, so that Lee's body lay in state outside the Studio where for so many years Lee had taught and lectured his actors, sometimes sternly, but always with deep love and concern.

I remember Cheryl leaning against the iron gate outside the Actors Studio, shaking her head, heart-broken, as she stared at the hearse that bore Lee's body.

A few years later, when Cheryl died, the actors met at the Studio, mournfully, to memorialize her. Asked to address them, I told them Cheryl's story of Lee speaking to the Group Theatre and reminding them, "This is a play about idealism and you are idealists! That is why you are here." And I commented, "Cheryl carried that idealism under her heart and gave it to you here in the Actors Studio, and you have inherited that dream, and that is why you are here—and don't you ever forget it."

❏

# Cecil Beaton
## BY
# Tammy Grimes

There he was, this exquisite looking man—beautiful features, particularly his thin aquiline nose, all perfectly set on a rather small, nobly shaped head—white hair a bit longer than most I remember (but not *one* hair out of place). There he sat, alone, in a dark suit, high white starched collar, with a star-like light from a low-ceilinged gray wall shining down on him in a popular cabaret, The Upstairs at the Downstairs, in New York City. Cecil Beaton, a connoisseur of good taste with an endless knowledge of the finest songs.

Mr. Beaton came to see the second performance of my first cabaret. He was the costume designer for *Look After Lulu*—the title role of which Noel Coward had offered to me only the night before. I didn't, at that age, fathom Mr. Beaton's universal fame nor his accomplishments—universally known as a set and costume designer in the opera, ballet, film, and theatre world, not to mention his fame as a renowned photographer.

I approached his table in my deep red rose-patterned slip of a dress, my blond hair piled high on my head, a few curls swirling here and there—this man unraveled effortlessly upwards to his full height of 6'3" or more to greet me. The first statement I heard from his lips was, "Miss Grimes, may I say, you have the most untidy hair I have ever seen." This was my very first *costume designer* and my very first Broadway show to be *directed* by Cyril Ritchard. Feydeau's farce, adapted by Noel Coward to become *Look After Lulu*.

Then:

C.B.  What are your favorite colors?

T.G.  Black, beige, Italian red, pale pink, variations of peach colors, lavender, deep purple and green—love *Forest Green*. HATE WHITE, Hate high collars, Hate YELLOW, and bright ANYTHING except gold.

C.B.  You may have a pale pink chiffon nightgown with lavender straps. You *will* have a Chinese YELLOW heavy satin peignoir over the nightgown and I shall paint purple irises on the border—a green suit and veiled hat is fine with me.

T.G.  No Yellow—No High Collar!

C.B.  (Laconically) Wait and see.

At times he worked for days or more on just one dress—I stood for hours and hours stone-still as he placed a hand-made chiffon orchid under and to the left of my breast—slightly-this-way, slightly-that-way, up, down, sideways until he was satisfied, tacking-untacking with tiny pins—every pleat—every fold—every button, bow, sleeve, pucker, hem-line, train—every single part of each costume was touched by those nimble fingers. When he dipped his brushes and began to paint there emerged this border of irises, their green stalks and graceful leaves bending between the folds of that glorious material, the color of the blazing sun.

During the creation of each gown my eyes would catch the workers who seemed almost like elves to me, crouched and moving round my body as Cecil spoke to them—quickly darting from place to place, moving a quarter of an inch there or up a half, they finally straightened up after hours on their knees as Cecil called: "*Thank you*—Good day's work," and they rose with glowing faces at the "Master's" praise, and the doors of the famous establishment of Madame Karinska's were bolted once more until early the next morning.

I remember, in particular, the set Cecil designed for *Lulu* (the bedroom for Roddy McDowall's character)—the wall-paper was simply one nude after another of Brigitte Bardot in all her glory—*Marvelous!! That was Cecil!*

I remember waltzing round and round and round with Cecil in an oval candle-lit ballroom of a friend's home under a beautifully painted ceiling, his long black cape swirling, head high, hand on the small of my back almost lifting me off the floor—This was Cecil's world. I believe he knew how much respect and delight I had in being with him on a few such occasions—with stories, walking—observing and often much laughter. One sensed something threatening—if provoked he could swiftly uncoil that piercing sarcasm.

I spent an afternoon at Cecil's Edwardian home in London—high ceilings painted pale yellow, sun streaming through the windows and roses everywhere—*That was Cecil!*

One day before *Lulu* closed he created a mock Edwardian set cut from cardboard in his studio where he photographed all of my costumes. The *last* photograph he took (which I think I cherish most) was of my head coming through what looked like a cracked egg breaking through a piece of cardboard—it is only as I begin to write about him now that I understand: he saw me as this freshly hatched chick seeing the world, and the theatre, for the first time. It was indeed the beginning of my career on Broadway, and as I have climbed that costume platform for fittings for many many years now, I often say: "You know, I was very spoiled as a young actress; my first costumes were designed by Cecil Beaton." Some know that name is a challenge for all of us to study our work with a magnifying glass.

Thank you, dear Cecil.

*On a train bound for*
*New Haven, Connecticut*     *1959*

# Tim Curry
## BY
# Ian McKellan

I knew Tim Curry in London, long before his worldwide fans discovered him. Admiring his histrionic talent for flamboyance and glamour, his fans may be surprised that, with his friends, he has always been mild-mannered and a little secretive. But in public, and private, he is constant in his wit and his generosity. I wish only one change in him—that he would come back home more often.

*Los Angeles*     *1991*

# Burt Reynolds
## BY
# Dinah Shore

Burt is loyal, sensitive, talented, honorable, impetuous, thoughtful—I could go on and on but if these admirable qualities make him sound like Mr. Perfect and therefore a little dull—I assure you, he is anything but! (As if you didn't know.) And there's that wonderfully oblique sense of humor—he's fun and funny and to my educated eye—very dear.

*Studio City, California*        *1992*

# Wendy Hiller
## BY
# Sir John Gielgud

I first got to know Wendy Hiller when I directed her in a production of *The Cradle Song* in 1952, and we have been devoted friends ever since. We have acted together most happily in a number of plays, films, and on television. An indomitable worker, generous colleague and inspiring professional actress, it is difficult to do justice in a few words to the wide range of talents which she possesses. With her fresh, vigorous approach, her endlessly unselfish, sympathetic attitude towards all who have the privilege of working with her, she embodies a personality which is utterly steadfast and adorable.

*Los Angeles       1991*

# Mary Steenburgen
## BY
# Christine Lahti

When I first met Mary Steenburgen I knew she was very talented, I'd heard how sweet and kind she was, but what really surprised me was this rowdy, raucous, gritty laughter that kept erupting out of her. I've also discovered that Mary may well be the most centered and healthy actress I know. Her priorities in life all make sense—her family and friends really are sometimes more important than her career, and always at least as important. I respect her acting talent tremendously, but it is her talent for living that even gets to me more. In our "show-biz" world of effusiveness and hype, Mary is the real thing—the genuine article. She inspires me, moves me, and makes me laugh—a lot. I believe our friendship will have a very long run.

*Ojai, California*    *1990*

# Joseph Schildkraut
## BY
# Francis Lederer

My acquaintance with Pepi Schildkraut started shortly after my arrival in Hollywood. One day I received a telegram welcoming me which I believed to be a very kind and generous gesture from somebody whom I had known only by name. I had seen Pepi several times on the screen before I arrived at the movie capital, and I remember him first of all for his breathtaking masculine beauty in his starring parts in American pictures. His name was primarily known to me because of his father, Rudolf Schildkraut. Ah! Ha! If anybody would have asked me who in my opinion was the greatest actor in the world, I would have unhesitatingly said "Rudolf." I stood next to that Titan several times on the stage of the theatre in Prague, where I was a beginner, as he played Shylock in *The Merchant of Venice*. The reality and truth of his acting was so overwhelming that when the judge in the court scene challenged Shylock to cut a pound of flesh out of the arrogant Venetian playboy-aristocrat, Schildkraut sharpened his dagger on the bottom of his shoe as he was about to thrust it into his adversary's chest. I and all the others on the stage were so frightened that Shylock would do it at all of the performances.

Pepi's father, however, was against his son becoming an actor. He desired him to be a violinist. But Pepi wanted his father to be convinced of his talent, and asked him to attend one of his performances. When the curtain came down, his father went backstage and walked around his son thrusting contemptuous looks in his direction and finally said, "The tie is wrong, too."

Nevertheless, Pepi was fortunate to have inherited, through his father's genes, some of his talent. He became a very successful actor on the stage and in motion pictures, winning an Academy Award for his performance as Dreyfus in *The Life of Emile Zola* as well as a particularly gifted performance as Philippe Égalité in *Marie Antoinette*. In his later years he scored an enormous success on stage and in film with his haunting interpretation of Papa Frank in *The Diary of Anne Frank*. Personally, he was extremely kind and helped me tremendously when I replaced him in that part so that I could be successful in the role that he created with such distinction!

# Kevin Costner
## BY
# James Earl Jones

Kevin is a centered human being—centered in his ego so that he can look at a script and truly want to do all the roles, but unlike Bottom in *A Midsummer Night's Dream*, he needed not to. Instead, this healthy appreciation allows him to understand more deeply the task of his fellow actors. He is centered also in that he seems to have embraced this odd profession with his feet planted firmly on the ground, and does not get thrown by the power of others (artistic and otherwise), and is constantly defining his own power (artistic and otherwise). He is centered in his vision; he sees in all three hundred and sixty degrees. He sits in the middle of the creative experience, and sees it all for what it is worth: the actor's worth, the writer's worth, the director's worth and the story's worth. Without fear of mere flattery, I could call Kevin a "visionary."

*Los Angeles*       *1992*

# José Ferrer
## BY
# Richard Brooks

José Ferrer—actor, director, philosopher, friend, father, husband of two remarkable actresses, Uta Hagen and Rosemary Clooney.

He was a great Cyrano, ultimate professional, dedicated, generous, meticulous, funny, energetic, talented.

*Los Angeles*      *1983*

# Barry Humphries
## BY
# Alec Guinness

Barry Humphries—I don't much like gladioli, but I would cheerfully wave one in celebration of a unique talent. Talent? More than that. We have all gotten to know the ubiquitous Dame Edna and something of the ghastly Sir Les Patterson, but it is Sandy Stone who beguiles and moves me from the other side of the grave, and enlarges our sympathy for humankind.

*Los Angeles       1992*

# Alice Faye
## BY
# Ellen Burstyn

When I was a kid in Detroit, I collected movie star pictures from movie magazines and kept them in a big folder. When my friends came over, we'd "trade." They'd look at my pictures. I'd look at theirs, and then we'd say which ones we wanted to swap. But some we'd never trade for anything. I never traded my Alice Fayes. She was my favorite. I tried wearing my hair parted in the middle like hers, but it somehow didn't look as good on me as it did on her.

When we made *Alice Doesn't Live Here Anymore*, Marty Scorsese added the first scene which was Alice as a child. We decided Alice was named after Alice Faye, and we had the character Alice sing one of Alice Faye's songs. She was my idea of beauty and glamor. I still don't look good with my hair parted in the middle. But I bet she does, even now.

*Beverly Hills        1991*

# John Travolta

## BY

# Jim Bridges

*From my journal—January 20, 1992*

Roddy called yesterday and wanted to know if I was finished with the piece I agreed to write about Travolta for his new book. I panicked. Although I have made several attempts to write the damn thing, I have been having a lot of trouble trying to decide exactly what to say. At first I thought it would be easy. I've known John for a long time, but when I started trying to describe him, I remembered how Houseman had warned me about speaking in hyperboles. Then I thought, why don't I just type up some entries from my diaries over the years? I could include our first meeting in 1978 when Jane Fonda and I, during the shooting of *The China Syndrome*, invited John to lunch to discuss the possibility of our all doing a film together. (John, who loves to eat, was amused by our meager spread of tuna salad and cans of Vienna sausages, and invited us later to what he considered a properly catered affair.) Or how about something from the *Urban Cowboy* days? The first trip to Houston together on February 17, 1979, when I took him down to Gilley's to show him what the bar was like and to describe my vision of the film. (Rona Barrett had announced on television that John was going to be in there that night and the place was a madhouse.) The flight back to L.A., when he turned in his seat ahead of me and took my hand and said, "I want to be in your film." And our walk together after we landed when he said, "But you have to promise me one thing, if I'm not good in the movie, and you're not getting what you want, promise you'll fire me." The intensity with which he prepared for the role, learning the cowboy dances, riding the mechanical bull, the fight for Debra Winger, the shooting itself, which was tough and demanding and the most fun I ever had on a film. The post-production period when John would drop by and look at edited footage, the excitement when we saw the first cut on February 8, 1980, the big premiere in Houston when John was almost crushed in Gilley's by fans, the satisfaction of success. Or maybe I should write about the period of time after *Urban Cowboy* when John and I were looking for another film to do together. The disappointment and press misconception of our aborted *Chorus Line*. The afternoon we went to see Elizabeth Taylor in *The Little Foxes* (she was marvelous), going backstage, leaving the theater with her, opening the outside door to face hundreds of fans behind a police barricade screaming with excitement as they saw the two of them together. "It's her! Oh, my God, and him!" Or maybe I should pull out all the stuff on *Perfect*. The day Aaron Latham and I described the film to John and committed without a script, the days in New York doing research around *Rolling Stone* with John and Jann Wenner (it was John's idea that Jann should play himself), the days at the Sports Connection doing the research there, fighting for Jamie Lee Curtis, shooting with Gordon Willis, showing the first cut to John who wanted to see it alone, the excitement about the studio reception on December 20, 1984, the overly hostile critical response. It's really hard to decide. There are so many entries. John and I have been through so much together and throughout he has remained one of the nicest, most talented and positive people I have ever met. I wonder if Roddy will give me a couple more days to figure out which entries to use and/or what to say about this friend and superstar.

P.S. Or maybe I should rethink the piece and write about John and his airplanes (I rode with him once from Las Vegas to L.A. in a terrifying wind storm and he flew the plane with amazing skill). Or how about Kelly, his wife, and their adorable son Jett? Roddy, I need more time!

❏

# Elsa Lanchester
## BY
# Gavin Lambert

Childhood memory. The first time my parents took me to the theater, the play was *Peter Pan*; and it was Elsa, not Charles Laughton as Captain Hook, who frightened me. Flying at astonishing speed on wires, she became a tiny, demonic, red-crested bird of prey, far more dangerous than the entire pirate gang, who obviously didn't stand a chance against her.

Years later, when I told her so, Elsa explained that she had decided to play the part, much to the author's annoyance, as a Bad Seed. In her view, if Peter Pan had ever grown up, he would have turned into "a kind of Hitler." Elsa was also very pleased that Charles had left so little impression on me. (Hook, I suppose now, was one of the roles he never came to grips with.) She always enjoyed turning the tables on an audience, and it was an extra bonus to turn them on Charles as well.

If only, I used to think, Elsa had been lesbian, they might have become a couple as well matched as Vita Sackville-West and Harold Nicolson. But instead of arriving at a calm, solid affection outside sex, they played an angry bondage game for more than thirty years, alternating the roles of judge and victim, confidant and betrayer. On the stage, in the early years of their marriage, Elsa played Ariel to Charles's Prospero; in life, neither could set the other free.

Acting together in movies, they could be almost unnervingly effective as players in a power struggle. Elsa's Anne of Cleves in *The Private Life of Henry VIII*, unable to seduce her husband on their wedding night and intimidating him instead, is an ambiguous blend of eccentricity and cunning. *The Beachcomber*, although ineptly directed, has the same kind of performance tension, with Elsa as a prim but desperately coy missionary determined to reform Laughton's gloriously scruffy South Seas bum. Best of all is *Witness for the Prosecution*, their last appearance together, with Elsa playing "devoted" nurse to Laughton's testy invalid lawyer, trapped in their need to needle each other. It's only in *Rembrandt* that nothing seems to happen between them. Cardboard figures, equally ill at ease as Misunderstood Artist and Faithful Muse, neither can make us believe they are simply, happily in love.

But the best of Elsa, the really basic Elsa, is to be found elsewhere. In *The Bride of Frankenstein*, of course, whose director, James Whale, had the kind of bitter and extravagant humor that fully released her own. The Bride herself is grotesque and yet somehow pitiable, an apparition of sheer outrage, hair frizzed with anger, eyes flashing and mouth hissing with protest; but she is, literally, only the half of it. The movie also gives us Elsa as Mary Shelley, from whose unconscious the Bride sprang—an improbably demure and slyly innocent Victorian young lady.

"I am told," Elsa once remarked of her style as a cabaret artist, "that my innocent expression prior to my knowing smile is my number-one weapon." Basic Elsa goes back to her nightclub days in London during the 20s, a career that she revived in Hollywood twenty years later at the Turnabout Theater, and again during the 60s, when Charles directed her in a one-woman show that he called *Elsa Lanchester—Herself*. Here she established her own corner in Beatrice Lillie-Hermione Gingold territory, performing folksy-naughty songs that she punctuated with wide-eyed looks and sudden manic laughs. Her specialty was the double-entendre, and she had a rare collection. "If you can't get in the corners, you might as well give up," she sang as a maid with an inordinately long mop. Looking as demure as Mary Shelley, she announced, "If you go walking out without your hat pin, you may come home without your you-know-what." And as another maid, who got in the corners and married her employer: "Since Mr. Badger-Butts gave me his hyphen/I've never never never been the same/For I've found that when a lady has a hyphen/It changes more than just her name."

There were no sets, but Elsa managed to create, by gesture and movement, alone on a bare stage, what she called a "map." It was also a map of herself, quirky, flirtatious, acid, lewd, shrewd, and sometimes totally wacko.

*Los Angeles*       *1982*

# Donald Crisp
## BY
# Maureen O'Hara

"A few short words about Donald Crisp—that's all I need," Roddy said. What an impossible task he gave me. How can I write a few short words about such a man?

From the time he played General Grant in *Birth of a Nation*, Donald Crisp was a distinguished director, writer, actor, and a highly successful business entrepreneur and investor—a man loyal and proud of his predominantly Scottish and Irish roots. When he wanted to be nice to me he talked about his Irish roots, and when he wanted to tease me he lauded his Scottish roots.

We used to say, "Huh, he's more traditionally Scots than Irish," because he was stingy, I mean thrifty, beyond belief. Many of us thought he deliberately worked hard trying to create that impression—he succeeded. His stinginess impressed us. We loved him for it, and forgave him, as we chuckled over this beloved idiosyncrasy.

If he took us out to dinner we were permitted one beverage only because—"more than one is bad for your health." When my daughter Bronwyn was a wee girl, Donald became engaged to her. He gave her, as her "engagement" ring, the band off his cigar. When we were making *Spencer's Mountain*, in which he played Henry Fonda's father and my father-in-law, he arrived on the Jackson Hole, Wyoming location about 2 A.M. I worried about the fact that we would all be in bed, and the motel cafe would be closed when he arrived. So I bought a pretty tray, put some personal linen on it, my china plate with cookies and finger sandwiches, some fresh fruit, my precious teapot, some tea bags and my traveling hot water heater. I put it in his room with a welcome note. I never saw my possessions again—not even my teapot, and it had my initials on it! Later my curiosity made me query him about it, and he said, "Oh yes, thank you for the lovely gift!"

But—at night Donald would come to my room. We never went to his—we might order room service. He would sit on my rocking chair in the middle of the room. We would sit around him on the floor, and as he rocked back and forth he would hold us enthralled with his stories of his life, his career in the theatre, in movies, in Hollywood—stories about the people he knew, and the people he worked with, the people he respected, and the people he didn't respect. He never told us about his business life. He didn't want us to know how rich he really was!

I wish in those days we had the little recorders we have now. What a golden store is lost to us!

How I loved this warm, sweet, kind, wonderful, fascinating, stingy Scotsman. I miss him.

*New York City*      *1955*

# Irene Worth
## BY
# Lynn Redgrave

When I first started acting, I had all sorts of dreams. I believed that a great actor should be able to play any character at all, that no role should be considered wrong for them.

Over the years, I began to think that maybe this was unrealistic, until I saw Irene act.

Again and again Irene's characterizations push the casting boundaries. Irene has no age, and if I hadn't worked with her I wouldn't know if she was tall or short, dark or fair, English, American, German, Italian . . . you name it.

She can be anyone . . . and brilliantly.

She is a GREAT ACTOR. And when she is being Irene . . . she's witty and bright, perceptive and brilliant. A GREAT WOMAN.

*New York City*      *1960*

# Brandon de Wilde
## BY
# Patricia Neal

I will never forget the first time I saw Brandon de Wilde in a play. The play was *A Member of the Wedding*, starring Ethel Waters, Julie Harris and Brandon de Wilde. He was only seven years old at the time, but I will always remember thinking, "Wow! he's got it."

Many years later I had the opportunity to work with him in films. The first film we did was *Hud* starring Paul Newman. Oh! My goodness, Brandon had become quite a pro at the ripe old age of twenty. We got along famously, and we were lucky enough to repeat it again in Honolulu when we did *In Harm's Way*.

Sadly, we never had a chance to work together again. My dear Brandon was tragically killed in a car accident only a few years later.

As far as I am concerned, every fine, gifted, sensitive young actor now has his own patron saint.

*Los Angeles*        *1959*

# Swoosie Kurtz
## BY
# John Guare

Swoosie loves everything about restaurants. She loves to go to them. She loves to hold the menu and study it and have the waiter tell in great length about the evening's specials. She loves to order. She loves to look at the food when it comes. She just doesn't like to eat it. At the end of the evening, the waiter takes the table's dishes away but then returns to Swoosie with her uneaten dinner wrapped in silver. She takes the silver package home, puts a label on it with the date and jams it in her freezer. Swoosie's memoirs are in her refrigerator.

By the by. Swoosie's father named her after his WWII fighter plane that now hangs in the Smithsonian Institute: The Swoose—a swan and a goose.

Swoosie is a magician who belies Stanislavski.

During the run of my play *The House of Blue Leaves* (in which she scored a personal triumph and won a Tony) I'd sit in her dressing room and we'd yak away until curtain time. Then Beckler the Stage Manager would call "Places" and Swoosie would put on her wig and — I swear this is true — Swoosie would not be there anymore. All you saw leaving the dressing room was a shattered individual named Bananas who'd been broken by her husband's dreams of songwriting fame.

Two hours later she'd return to her dressing room, leaving a cheering audience devastated. She'd pull off her wig. Swoosie returned, smiling that smile. "So. Where do we eat?"

*Studio City, California*     *1991*

245

# Isaac Stern
## BY
# Agnes de Mille

If Isaac Stern were not one of this century's great violinists, he would be a politician of world renown. He has the concern, he has the voice, he speaks irresistibly. And, my God, he has the energy. He saved Carnegie Hall from the real estate wreckers who would have supplanted it with a parking facility. Had he had the time he would have saved that other great landmark, The Metropolitan Opera House. All matters interest him. But he is foremost a great musical virtuoso, and this quite properly engages the bulk of his time and strength. As part of his profession he also teaches, giving master classes around the world, and participating in very many educational projects dealing with music. Indeed, there are few good causes that he has not lent his name and working services to.

He is, above all, a loyal and devoted friend. Isaac Stern is a man of high integrity. Let us honor him. We do love him.

*Beverly Hills*          *1965*

# Michael Caine
## BY
# Roger Moore

If Michael Caine were writing this piece to accompany *my* picture he would say that, "This excellent photograph by Roddy McDowall is of an actor of considerable good looks, an exceeding abundance of charm, and one of the most underrated actors of our time and I am proud to be numbered amongst his very close friends." . . . so if Michael were to say that of me then I shall most certainly say it of him. If you should read this Michael, is there anything for me on your next?

*EDITOR'S NOTE:* On September 5, 1991 a memorial service was held for Coral Browne at the Farmers Church in London. A letter written by her husband, Vincent Price, was read by John Schlesinger and it is printed here, along with a remembrance written and delivered by Alan Bates.

Dear John:

When I was courting Coral, the first gift she gave me was a photo of herself simply signed: "Remember Coral"—not really a challenge as the problem was: how could you forget her? I've come to believe remembering someone is not the highest compliment—it is missing them. I find I miss every hour of Coral's life—I miss her morning cloudiness, noon mellowness, evening brightness. I miss her in every corner of our house, every crevice of my life. In missing her, I feel I'm missing much of life itself. Over her long illness, as I held her hand or stroked her brow, or just lay still beside her, it was not the affectionate contact we'd known as we wandered down the glamorous paths we'd been privileged to share in our few years together; we were marching towards the end of our time and we both knew it. But, in our looks, our smiles, the private, few, soft-spoken words, there was hope of other places, other ways, perhaps, to meet again.

One fact of Coral I'll always miss: her many, many devoted friends—many here, today, in this beautiful church, celebrating her life more than mourning her death, and missing the liveliness of her wit, her personal beauty, her outgoing self. I love them all for loving her. Many of you have shared more of her life than I have, but that very private and intense passion for her is mine alone.

She survived that last long year on the love of her friends, their caring and concern—and very especially yours, dear John. I miss you all, and though we may not meet as often, nor in the great good company of my wife, you are in my memory locked.

All my love,
Vincent

# Coral Browne
## BY
# Alan Bates

I can hear Coral now saying, "So you got stuck with the address, did you, darling, good luck; and don't think I won't be listening."

To sum up the life and spirit of Coral Browne in a short address is pretty impossible, but here goes. Her beloved, and much loved, husband, Vincent Price, has asked me not to tell a lot of legendary Coral Browne stories. And indeed most people here know them, and quite a few people here are the subject of them, so I couldn't tell them anyway; some of them were magnificently retold in her last notices (they were not obituaries, they were the best notices I have ever read for anyone, and rightly so).

We all knew Coral Browne the superb actress, witty, stylish, powerful, classical, and of course beautiful.

We all knew the Coral Browne that she presented to us socially, a great personality, mischievous, alarming, unpredictable, outrageous. It could be said that this "Coral Browne" was one of her great performances, one she certainly relished, and revelled in. I think there is another less well known Coral Browne. I was invited to present her Evening Standard Award for that superb performance in Dennis Potter's *Dreamchild*. I made a rather extravagant announcement as one does on these occasions, and she came to the stage, suddenly a Coral I had not reckoned with before. The supremely confident Coral Browne was nervous, she forgot the name of someone she thought highly of and very much wanted to thank, and was, in short, suddenly vulnerable. I think the reason why we all loved her was perhaps because we all sensed that underneath her wicked sense of humour was this vulnerability, and it made all her outrageousness wonderfully acceptable. She was kind, she was generous, she was loyal, she was extremely sensitive to other people's condition, their bereavements, and *their* vulnerability. She loved people—she could see right through us all, of course, and we loved her because she dared to say what she saw. Above all, she was brave, fearless in her defense of those she loved and cared for, and totally courageous in the period of her illness. A great example of these various qualities was evident in her encounter with Guy Burgess in Moscow—courage, compassion and understanding. It was a great privilege to share with her the retelling of this story, brilliantly presented by Alan Bennett and John Schlesinger.

If we have not had as much of Coral Browne the actress as we could, and would have liked to have had, it is for a very particular reason. She worked at her *life*; her relationships, her friendships and her marriages were *successful*. She was not *only* ambitious as an actress—she was a superb one and did quite enough work to establish that—Ardèle, *Waltz of the Toreadors*, *Hedda Gabler*, Regan, Goneril, Lady Macbeth, Mrs. Warren, Gertrude, *Dreamchild*, *The Sea*, *An Englishman Abroad*, *What the Butler Saw*, Emilia, Mrs. Erlynne—but living her life was important too. She loved travel, art, fashion, people and was totally curious about the world around her. I first knew her as the wife of my first agent, a lovely man, Phillip Pearman, whom she adored and nursed with great devotion when he was fatally ill. In later life she met and married Vincent Price; this is one of the great love affairs that we have witnessed, two witty, compassionate, intelligent, handsome people in late life showing us all how to do it, how to share a life. The eloquence with which Vincent expressed his love for Coral in the letter to John we've just heard is unforgettable.

If I cannot tell Coral Browne stories then I will tell two Vincent Price ones. Coral and Vincent came to see me in *A Patriot for Me* in Los Angeles. They took a few of us out for dinner. A woman came up to Vincent at the end of the meal and said, "Can I have your autograph," and he said "Certainly" and signed it "Dolores Del Rio" (the legendary silent film actress). I said, "Vincent, you cannot do that—she'll be back in a rage in a minute. She'll pour a bowl of soup over your head." He turned to me solemnly and said, "Before she died, Dolores said to me, 'Don't *ever* let them forget me'; so now I always sign Dolores Del Rio." Perhaps we should always now sign our autographs "Coral Browne." Don't let us ever let them forget her.

Before she was confined to bed, I rang up to speak to Coral; Vincent picked up the phone: "She's gone to confession," he said, "and she's going to be an *awful* long time." Just two stories which, when you know Coral and her stories, show you what fun they must have had together.

When I think of the alarm one always felt when leaving a party before Coral, at what she might be saying about oneself, it makes me wonder now that *she* has left the party first, what she is saying to the powers that be; if she's true to form we'll never get in! Or perhaps it is simply that we will have no need for confession ourselves—we will just have to say, "Anything you wish to know about me, please refer my case to Coral Browne."

What a woman, what a character, what an actress, what pleasure we have had in her company, our very own Australian, English-Woman-Abroad.

God bless you, Coral.

# Index

❏